OECD Studies on Water

Reforming Sanitation in Armenia

TOWARDS A NATIONAL STRATEGY

This work is published under the responsibility of the Secretary-General of the OECD. The opinions expressed and arguments employed herein do not necessarily reflect the official views of OECD member countries.

This document and any map included herein are without prejudice to the status of or sovereignty over any territory, to the delimitation of international frontiers and boundaries and to the name of any territory, city or area.

Please cite this publication as:
OECD (2017), *Reforming Sanitation in Armenia: Towards a National Strategy*, OECD Studies on Water, OECD Publishing, Paris.
http://dx.doi.org/10.1787/9789264268982-en

ISBN 978-92-64-26899-9 (print)
ISBN 978-92-64-26898-2 (PDF)

Series: OECD Studies on Water
ISSN 2224-5073 (print)
ISSN 2224-5081 (online)

Foreword

The objective of this study is to support the development of a Strategy on Sustainable Sanitation Sector Development and Construction of wastewater treatment plants (WWTPs) for Armenia. It was conducted by the OECD within the framework of the National Policy Dialogue on Water Policy in Armenia in co-operation with the European Union Water Initiative (EUWI) facilitated by the OECD and UNECE. The work was financially supported by the European Union.

The study was designed to identify options to increase the coverage of the Armenian population connected to wastewater collection and treatment in a financially realistic way. It includes a specific focus on sanitation services in Armenia, as these have been relatively neglected until recently.

The present study was conducted in three stages:

- Stage 1 set the stage for the assignment, reviewed the policy, legal and regulatory framework for sanitation services in Armenia, evaluated the current levels of service, identified future investment needs and assessed expected developments.

- Stage 2 set out recommendations for reforms, with alternative options to organise and finance sanitation services in Armenia, particularly in terms of the scale and scope of those services and alternative options for raising tariffs for sanitation, where applicable. These recommendations were presented in a workshop in Yerevan on 1 April 2014.

- Stage 3 formulated a strategy for sustainable sanitation in Armenia based on all analysis conducted during previous stages and feedback received at the workshop. The present synthesis report captures all findings and recommendations formulated in previous stages of the assignment and identifies the needs for further work and assistance to effectively support water authorities in the development and implementation of a national strategy for sanitation.

Acknowledgements and disclaimer

The project was implemented as part of the National Policy Dialogue (NPD) on water policy in Armenia conducted in co-operation with the European Union Water Initiative (EUWI) in Eastern Europe, Caucasus and Central Asia and facilitated by the OECD and the United Nations Economic Commission for Europe (UNECE).

The OECD commissioned Trémolet Consulting Limited (UK) jointly with JINJ Ltd. (Armenia), which included Sophie Trémolet, Lilit Melikyan, Kevin Tayler, Eduard Mesropyan and Aida Iskoyan, for the analytical work. They are authors of this report. Tatiana Efimova at the OECD provided essential oversight and inputs into the project and this report.

The authors gratefully acknowledge the contribution of participants of the EUWI National Policy Dialogue to the project and to this report, and would like to thank the State Committee of Water Systems of Armenia for a very productive co-operation. The authors thank Xavier Leflaive (OECD) for his valuable comments that helped improve both the content and structure of the report, and express their appreciation to Matthew Griffiths (OECD) for professional contributions to the project at its final stage. In addition, the authors thank Shukhrat Ziyaviddinov, Maria Dubois and Lupita Johanson (all OECD), for their valuable contribution to preparing publication of the report.

This report has been developed within the framework of The European Union Water Initiative (EUWI) funded by the European Union, implemented by the OECD in partnership with UNECE. The views presented in this report are those of the authors and can in no way be taken to reflect the official opinion of the Government of Armenia, the European Union, or the OECD and its member countries.

Table of contents

Figures

Tables

Abbreviations and acronyms

AMD	Armenian Dram
ANSF	Armenian National Sanitation Fund
ASIF	Armenian Social Investment Fund
ASHMS	Armenian State Hydro Metrological Service
AWHHE	Armenian Women for Health and Healthy Environment
AWSC	Armenian Water and Sewerage Company
BMP	Basin Management Plan
CFOA	Community Finance Officers Association
CIS	Commonwealth of Independent States
CJSC	Closed Joint Stock Company
DFID	Department for International Development (UK)
EBRD	European Bank for Reconstruction and Development
FINCA	Foundation for International Community Assistance
FSU	Former Soviet Union
GDP	Gross Domestic Product
GoA	Government of Armenia
HOA	Home Owners Association
HTS	Hydrotechnical structure
IFC	International Finance Corporation
IFI	International Financing Institution
ILCS	Integrated Living Conditions Survey
IMC	Inter-municipal co-operation
IWRM	Integrated Water Resource Management
JBIC	Japan Bank for International Co-operation
JMP	Joint monitoring programme
KfW	KreditanstaltfürWiederaufbau (Germany)

LC	Lease Contract
LMABM	Law on Multi Apartment Building Management
LSGB	Local Self Government Body
MABMB	Multi Apartment Building Management Bodies
MC	Management Contract
MOH	Ministry of Health
MNP	Ministry of Nature Protection
MTA	Ministry of Territorial Administration
MTEF	Medium Term Expenditure Framework
NDP	National Development Plan
NGO	Non-Governmental organization
NPD	National Policy Dialogue
NWC	National Water Council
NSS	National Statistics Service
NWP	National Water Programme
OECD	Organisation for Economic Co-operation and Development
O&M	Operation and Management
PFBP	Poverty Family Benefit Programme
PPP	Public Private Partnership
PSP	Private Sector Participation
PSRC	Public Services Regulatory Commission
RDF	Regional Development Fund
RoA	Republic of Armenia
SCWS	State Committee for Water Systems
SEI	State Environmental Inspectorate
SGMC	Hydrogeological Monitoring Centre
SHAEI	State Hygiene and Anti-Epidemiological Inspectorate
SNCO	State Non-Commercial Organization
SWC	State Water Cadastre
SWCIS	State Water Cadastre Information System
UNDP	United Nations Development Programme
UNECE	United Nations Economic Commission for Europe
USAID	United States Agency for International Development

USD	United States Dollar
WB	World Bank
WBMA	Water Basin Management Agency
WFD	Water Framework Directive
WRMA	Water Resources Management Agency
WSC	Water and sewerage company
WSS	Water and sanitation service
WSUP	Water Systems Use Permit
WUA	Water User Associations
WUP	Water Use Permit
WWTP	Wastewater treatment plant
Yerevan Jur WSC	Yerevan Water and Sewerage Company

The exchange rate used in this report is: 1 EUR = 544 Armenian Dram (AMD) as of 30 July 2013.

Executive summary

Armenia's sanitation services are inadequate. In rural areas, over half of the population use unimproved facilities, causing direct damage to the environment and exposing inhabitants to health risks. In urban areas, the situation is substantially better, with 96% of the population having access to improved facilities through the sewerage system. Yet, this figure hides the poor conditions of the network, which poses health hazards due to potential cross-contamination between sewage and drinking water. Furthermore, out of 20 existing wastewater treatment plants (WWTPs), only four are currently functioning.

The need for a staged approach to investment

According to preliminary estimates, EUR 2.6 billion investments will be required to meet Armenia's sanitation needs, with approximately EUR 1 billion needing to be spent in the next 7 to 10 years. These additional investments would generate an approximate EUR 52 million additional operation and maintenance costs per year.

Given the country's current economic situation, this investment will have to be spread over time. In order to avoid further deterioration of infrastructure and increase of the financing gap, the need is for a targeted approach that focuses first on areas of greatest need and/or those that offer the best benefit to cost ratio and then proceeds in incremental steps towards overall goals. Sensible approaches, which provide for a range of interventions, should be developed in order to create favourable conditions and attract financial resources to the sector.

Improving Armenia's sanitation systems dictates a "Let's clean today as much as we can" approach. It also requires adopting auxiliary reforms to the market structure in order to increase the efficiency and quality of sanitation service delivery, to the financing arrangements so as to generate additional funds for sanitation and to the legal framework.

As the ultimate decision on how to manage water and sanitation services rests with territorial units, the given analysis recommends adopting a mix of "top-down" and "bottom-up" approaches. The central government should avoid "forcing" a market structure change on local governments. Rather, it should seek to create appropriate financial incentives designed to encourage and facilitate the changes that it deems appropriate.

Public funding will be needed going forward, particularly for new investments. Transfers from central to local governments are generally very limited, which means that local governments have very weak financing capacity, including for sanitation. There are a number of development funds that local governments could potentially approach in order to obtain funding for their sanitation projects.

An alternative to using existing (or planned) financing channels would be to create a dedicated fund for sanitation. Even with the establishment of the Regional Development Fund (RDF), there is a significant risk that funding for sanitation would be "lost" in the vast list of infrastructure needs. A proposed separate fund for sanitation, the Armenian National Sanitation Fund (ANSF) would focus on rural areas. The fund would need to pull funding from domestic public funding sources and donors but could also attract other investments from private investors or social foundations. Specific taxes could be earmarked to the fund. It would support local governments in investing in wastewater disposal and other sanitation services.

Support and assistance to commercial banks and microfinance finance institutions could help leverage private sources of finance for the sanitation sector. The Government should establish procedures for commercial banks' lending to communities in order to fully legitimise the process.

Develop a strong information base on sanitation services

An inventory of water and sanitation management arrangements for each territorial unit in the country should be prepared to inform reforms of the sanitation sector. This should include:

- Existing forms of sanitation services: What services are provided in the locality (water, on-site sanitation, sewerage services) and by which legal entities? Etc.

- For sewerage services: What is the number of sewerage connections, the length and diameter of sewerage pipes and their state of repair? What are the costs of service provision and how are those costs financed? Etc.

- For on-site services: which types of on-site sanitation facilities are in place? How much did these facilities cost and who has paid for them? How much have households invested themselves and did they get any financial support for doing so? What is the likely prevalence of illegal dumping in the area?

The National Statistical Service should also be encouraged to strengthen their surveys, so as to improve statistics on the volume of wastewater discharged without pre-treatment, include a separate question in the annual household survey to reflect household expenditure on water and sanitation

Define a sanitation-specific strategy with a related action-plan

It is recommended to prepare a sanitation-specific national strategy on sustainable sanitation. An alternative, least preferred option would be to amend the existing water policy to reflect sanitation priorities. The strategy should cover the following:

- Present a summary evaluation of the national context and current problems.

- Define targets in terms of sanitation coverage and levels of service at all steps of the value chain, based on a financial analysis of likely investment needs together with an evaluation of where funding is likely to come from.

- Further define the legal and regulatory framework on sanitation, wastewater collection, sludge treatment, treated wastewater and sludge reuse.

- Develop and adopt economic incentives for wastewater treatment process.

- Revise the method for calculating charges related to the discharge of treated wastewater into surface water basins.

Reflect the strategy into the legal and contractual frameworks

The national sanitation strategy will provide a basis for recommended approach, which will tackle the aspects that might have emerged during the development of the strategy, reforming the legal framework for sanitation i.e. developing a unified and comprehensive legal act to regulate the sanitation sector. As mentioned above, this could be done through a separate legal Act or through a new Chapter in the Water Code of the Republic of Armenia.

Chapter 1

The state of sanitation services in Armenia, reform objectives and investment needs

This chapter presents the current state of sanitation services in Armenia including environmental impact. It considers the status of sanitation services for rural and urban communities and residential, commercial and industrial users and also forecasts trends on the demand and supply side. The chapter considers the adequacy of service and operational considerations throughout the sanitation supply chain from collection, to treatment and discharge and reuse. This chapter analyses the investment needs for the sanitation sector in Armenia and considers objectives such as achieving universal coverage with "improved" sanitation and investment in new wastewater treatment facilities. It also considers the need for strategic investment to mitigate deterioration of existing infrastructure.

Overall reform objectives

The review of the existing situation highlighted the fact that the sanitation sector is currently under-prioritised in Armenia. As a result, infrastructure that was providing services during the Soviet era is now completely dilapidated and beyond repair, resulting in unsanitary conditions and environmental degradation. A consensus urgently needs to be built on the need to prioritise sanitation issues so that suitable policy reforms can be adopted and necessary investments can be made.

All stages of the sanitation value chain need to be improved through targeted investments and accompanying reform support measures. Those investments should enable the country to meet future Sustainable Development Goals (SDGs) and EU regulations within a time frame to be determined, taking account of overall availability of financial resources. Improvements should be set as clearly defined objectives, with an associated timeline and identified financial resources.

According to the initial assessment, investments are needed to achieve the following objectives.

- *Achieve universal coverage with improved sanitation services within a timeframe to be determined.* Given local factors such as the mountainous terrain and population dispersion, universal "sewerage" coverage is neither realistic nor affordable. As a result, appropriate standards for "improved sanitation" need to be defined for Armenia that are acceptable to the population, guarantee hygienic conditions and are affordable. Standards for improved faecal sludge management should also be developed and promoted, with particular emphasis placed on facilitating collection, transport and re-use of the faecal sludge produced by such facilities.

- *Invest in wastewater treatment, with the construction of new wastewater treatment facilities.* Given the high costs of wastewater treatment, particular emphasis needs to be placed on investing in wastewater treatment in pollution "hotspots" (areas with a combination of more densely populated areas, industrial discharges and limited receiving water capacity) and via decentralised and local treatment solutions that have low energy consumption or emphasise energy recovery. These types of solutions need to be carefully documented and assessed, with technical and financial support provided to WSCs and local governments for dissemination and adoption.

- *Promote re-use of treated wastewater for irrigation.* This will require the adoption of accompanying measures, such as changes to the legal framework to relax wastewater re-use standards.

- *Promote re-use of appropriately treated faecal sludge from on-site sanitation facilities.* This will require identifying uses for the treated faecal sludge, developing effective business models and assessing potential consumer resistance.

To achieve environmental improvements, it will also be necessary to ensure that all entities generating wastewater, including industrial users, commercial users and agri-business, apply an adequate approach to the removal of their wastewater, providing partial treatment if wastewater is discharged to sewers or full treatment if the treated wastewater is discharged to the water basin. This calls for legal reforms and stronger enforcement of existing/new regulations, as enforcement has been a key area of weakness in the sanitation sector. Special attention should be paid to ensuring pre-treatment of heavily polluting industrial flows prior to discharge to sewers.

In order to enable those investments to take place, reforms will be needed to modify the current organisation and financing arrangements for the sector. These reforms will enable efforts to generate economies of scale and scope, move towards sustainable cost recovery for the sanitation sector, ensure equitable access by all and identify solutions that work for the poorest and most remote communities.

The objectives of the reforms can be summarised as follows:

- Generate economies of scale and scope and reduce both investment and operational costs for the efficient delivery of sanitation services.

- Move towards sustainable cost recovery for the sanitation sector, by identifying how much funding can be mobilised from within the sector and how much external transfers are required.

- Ensure equitable access by all and identify solutions that work for the poorest and most remote communities.

However, financing needs for the sector are immense, close to EUR 2.8 billion in total, as sanitation has been grossly under-prioritised and underfunded in the last decades. Following the policy discussions in Yerevan with key stakeholders of the sanitation sector in Armenia, it was deemed necessary to propose a realistic approach to meet these investments, staged in different phases over the next 30 years, to identify additional sources of financing for the sector and spell out the main areas where reforms to the legal framework are needed.

Access to sanitation in Armenia

Residential

In urban areas, access to improved sanitation is high. Yet, 4% of urban population do not have improved sanitation facilities. The urban population in large cities (particularly Yerevan) is expected to increase, thereby increasing the need to expand access to sewerage to urban populations.

This situation contrasts with that of rural areas, as half of Armenia's rural population (51%) use unimproved facilities. Unimproved sanitation facilities increase the risk of groundwater contamination, which is significant as 96% of Armenia's drinking water supply comes from groundwater sources or springs.

Approximately 830 of the 930 territorial units have no sewerage services and rely on on-site sanitation solutions. Some of these on-site facilities discharge directly into rivers, polluting surface water bodies. Local governments that are in charge of providing sanitation services have not created dedicated services to supervise and service on-site sanitation facilities Since building wastewater networks in mountainous areas can be prohibitively expensive, on-site sanitation solutions will remain necessary for years to come. However, it is necessary to develop appropriate solutions for on-site sanitation.

According to the GoA's strategy on the balanced development of the regions, equitable development calls for positive discrimination of communities lagging behind in terms of government and development partners funding. Rural communities are often poor and marginalised and specific support systems should be put in place to help them to address their sanitation needs.

Non-residential

A potentially large number of industrial and commercial users are not connected to the sewerage networks and discharge untreated sewage into water bodies. The pollution load of wastewater discharged is not clearly identified and monitored, and existing enforcement mechanisms are not effective. This creates negative environmental impacts, degrading the state of surface water bodies and harming biodiversity, including in the Lake Sevan area.

Industrial growth, particularly of polluting industries and agribusiness, will drive an increase in the volume of wastewater discharged directly to water bodies. This trend will aggravate environmental degradation.

Types of wastewater systems

Wastewater systems are designed for the removal of wastewater generated in settlements, industrial, commercial, public and recreational facilities. Collected wastewater can then be treated to the required level and discharged into surface water bodies or to the environment, or reused for different purposes.

There are two main types of wastewater collection system:

Combined, when storm water in the settlement area is removed together with municipal wastewater (household and industrial). Some multiple of the dry weather flow (typically three) is routed to the WWTP but storm flows in excess of this are discharged untreated to drains and water bodies through storm water overflows.

Fully separate, when two closed wastewater networks are planned independent on each other: the first for household and industrial wastewater and the second for storm water. In practice, some storm water may find its way into the nominally foul water sewers.

Sewage collection and treatment systems may be:

Centralised: these are used for receiving wastewater generated in settlements in an organised manner, removing it from the settlement area and treating it to the required level in a single large wastewater treatment plant.

Decentralised, in which different districts inside the same settlement implement wastewater removal through different wastewater systems operating independently from each other to different wastewater treatment plants.

Wastewater systems involve a complex of pipelines for wastewater collection and removal, manholes and inspection chambers to allow access to the sewers, pumping stations to lift wastewater and engineered structures for removal of gross solids and sediment, treatment and utilisation of the wastewater and treatment and utilisation of the sludge generated during treatment.

Treatment, discharge and reuse in Armenia

The wastewater treatment process consists of a sequence of technological cycles. The main cycles are the following:

Preliminary treatment, during which grit is removed and gross solids contained in the sewage flow are caught on screens and removed from the flow.

Primary treatment of wastewater, during which solids contained in the sewage flow that can settle are separated by gravity in sedimentation tanks. These solids include organic or inorganic particles, sand and other substances of mineral origin.

Biological treatment often referred to as secondary treatment of wastewater. For this process oxygen is required, therefore the process is carried out with artificial or natural aeration. In some cases, this phase may also include other auxiliary activities designed to achieve nitrification and denitrification, which contribute to the reforming of the contained organic compounds of nitrogen into nitrates, as well as to disrupting of nitrates with nitrogen gas separation, removal of dissolved salts of phosphorus. Biological treatment is normally followed by a further physical settling stage, during which solids created by biological activity in the treatment unit are allowed to settle so that they can be removed or returned to the head of the treatment plant.

Advanced treatment often referred to as tertiary treatment of wastewater, during which further biological treatment is carried out to further reduce the oxygen demand of the wastewater. This stage is mainly applied when the treated wastewater is discharged into water bodies of fishery or equivalent importance.

Sludge treatment and utilisation, during which sediment and sludge generated as a result of sedimentation and biological treatment of wastewater is treated (dewatering, stabilisation and digestion). In some cases, depending on the quantity of sludge and the treatment technology, biogas (methane) released as a result of digestion can be collected and used for energy purposes. In some cases when wastewater does not contain heavy metals and meets the requirements for agricultural fertilisers, it can be bagged after additional treatment and used as organic fertiliser for agricultural lands.

Each of these stages may be accompanied by a number of additional and/or supportive measures or sub-stages, such as physico-chemical treatment, application of chemical reagents, disinfection of treated wastewater, etc., depending on the level of wastewater contamination.

Out of 20 existing WWTPs, only four are currently functioning, serving Yerevan, Gavar, Martuni and Vardenis. Furthermore, these WWTPs only provide treatment (preliminary treatment and primary settling), with limited beneficial impact for the environment.

This means that 48% of wastewater is discharged in the environment without treatment and does not correspond to discharge standards (norms). The volume of untreated wastewater has been rapidly growing in recent years. Untreated wastewater is commonly used for irrigation, with no control of health risks. The situation is rendered possible as there are no requirements for wastewater treatment in the WSCs' contracts. There currently is no permanent solution for dealing with the residual sludge from treatment. Sludge releases methane, which is not captured or used in any way.

Similarly, there are no solutions for dealing with sludge from on-site sanitation solutions. This sludge is disposed-off in an ad-hoc manner with no treatment or reuse.

The quality and quantity of industrial wastewater discharges are not adequately monitored. In the case of fisheries, for example, the exact impact of these discharges on the environment needs to be better assessed.

Improvements in treatment and reuse services are needed in response to climate change and increased energy prices. As energy prices are set to increase, energy-efficient wastewater treatment solutions need to be found. In addition, efforts to develop options for re-use of sludge for energy production should be supported. Climate change will also reduce availability of water for irrigation whilst increasing the need for irrigation water. Treated wastewater may help fill the gap between demand and available supply.

Finally, environmental protection and approximation of EU Directives calls for increasing wastewater treatment levels with the objective of restoring the quality of water bodies.

Transport services, i.e. transport of wastewater via sewers and desludging services (for on-site sanitation facilities), are not operating adequately at present. About 50% of existing sewerage networks are in need of replacement – more than 80% in Yerevan and Shirak alone. Poor sewer condition creates health risks, with cross-contamination from sewers to drinking water supplies. Desludging services are provided mostly by small private enterprises, with limited involvement from the WSCs and no involvement from local governments.

Although there has been some isolated rehabilitation of sewer pipes as part of broader water investment projects, there has not been a comprehensive programme to rehabilitate sewerage pipes.

With the urban population in large cities (particularly Yerevan) expected to increase, sewerage rehabilitation and expansion in growing urban centres appears urgent. In addition, if a larger number of industrial users connect to the sewerage network, there will be a need to increase its carrying capacity. It is also likely that climate change will increase the frequency and intensity of flooding events, which are currently putting additional pressure on the network.

Applicable technologies for wastewater treatment in Armenia

WWTPs using conventional technologies

These plants are mainly intended/used for treatment of wastewater of relatively large settlements or group of settlements with a large population. These WWTPs are planned for full wastewater treatment for all the treatment cycles mentioned above. In this type of plant, treatment is carried out in reinforced concrete structures. The degree of treatment provided must be sufficient to meet national and local standards for the discharge of BOD, COD, suspended solids, nitrates, phosphates and other harmful substances to water basins.

Such plants have quite high-energy consumption and are expensive technologies. Their operation and maintenance requires qualified personnel. It is desirable that such plants are operated by a professional organisation.

Conventional wastewater treatment plants are constructed from concrete and incorporate separate units, with some space between them to allow for access and, in the case of circular units, geometry. For smaller plants, careful design can reduce the space requirement by designing units to fit within one overall structure. This is particularly appropriate for units such as sequencing batch reactors, which combine more than one stage in the sequence of treatment operations in one unit. The single structure approach is likely to be most appropriate for smaller plants, those with capacities in the range 5 000 to 30 000 m³/day.

Pre-fabricated compact treatment plants

These plants are manufactured in factory conditions. Most package plants are of this type. They are assembled in a frame of materials on metal or polymer-base, which allows the manufacturer to transport the fabricated plant by transport means from the manufacturer to the installation place. Such plants do not require large spaces and are easily operated.

In these plants, wastewater treatment is based on the same conventional technologies as those used for conventional treatment. Sludge treatment can be performed in different ways depending on the plant capacity, quantity of sludge, land availability and the demand for reuse of the treated sludge.

Pre-fabricated compact wastewater treatment plants (CWWTP) have a wide range of application: they are manufactured for treatment of 0.5 cubic m³/day to 5 000 m³/day wastewater flows.

They can be divided into two types, as follows:

- Container type CWWTPs, which are mainly made of metal elements coated with an anticorrosive layer and are designed for 50 m³/day to 5 000 m³/day wastewater treatment. The container-type CWWTPs are normally installed over ground and cover a small space. The entire wastewater treatment process is performed inside the container, in individual divisions for treatment stages. In terms of energy consumption, these plants are very close to the conventional type WWTPs. For their operation and maintenance, qualified personnel are also required. It is desirable that operation and maintenance of this type of plants is carried out by a specialised company.

- Module-type CWWTPs, which are mainly made of polymer-based materials and are designed for 0.5/day to 60 cubic m³/day wastewater treatment, which is equivalent to wastewater quantity generated from 3 to 300 inhabitants. The module-type CWWTPs are normally installed over ground and cover a very small space, and can be successfully harmonised with the area's landscape. The entire wastewater treatment process is performed inside the module. Some of these plants can provide rather high degree of wastewater treatment and have small demand of power. The simplicity of operation allows organising the plant operation by community inhabitants. A professional organisation is required only for maintenance.

WWTPs using alternative technologies

Wastewater treatment using alternative technologies is appropriate for rural and urban areas, which have relatively small number of population and a centralised sewerage system.

They include the following:

- Septic tanks, enclosed brick or concrete tanks in which solids settle and digest. These provide only primary treatment and must be followed with either a soak away or some form of secondary treatment.

- Waste stabilisation ponds, typically 1-2 metres deep, which rely on natural aeration. They are simple but require a large land area relative to other treatment options and are therefore likely to be most appropriate for treatment of waste from small isolated villages, where land is available.

- Aerated lagoons, typically around 3 metres deep although depths vary, with artificial aeration using air bubbles or a floating mechanical aerator.

- Constructed wetlands in which reeds and other plants are grown. Wastewater flows through the wetland, normally horizontally although there are also vertical flow wetlands and is treated by a combination of filtration and plant activity.

- Mixed solutions with combination of the above-mentioned options.

Biological lagoons are preferable in the regions where there is a deficit of irrigation water and the treated wastewater can be reused for irrigation, if needed. In this case, nitrates contained in household wastewater are a very good fertiliser. These points to the important principle that the treatment method should be chosen to suit where and how the treated waste water is to be discharged or reused.

Sludge can be dewatered in planted or unplanted drying beds.

The power demand of these alternative technological options, apart from aerated lagoons, is very low, and operation and maintenance is rather simple. Individuals without a professional background, but with corresponding technical training, can carry out operation. However, even the simplest treatment system will fail if basic operation and maintenance tasks are neglected.

Depending on the wastewater treatment requirements, it is possible to carry out also tertiary treatment. Wastewater can pass sequentially through the first, second and third degree biological ponds that will provide deeper treatment and the last pond can be used also for fishery purposes. Before discharging into water basins, treated wastewater can be drained in natural ground filters, on the surface of which permanent green areas will be created.

Improved individual pit toilets

In some cases, depending on the geographical location and the relief of the settlement, geological and hydrogeological characteristics of the area, the density of housing, number of population and social conditions, construction of a centralised wastewater removal and treatment system for the entire residential area or for a part (district) of it may be either unaffordable or undesirable.

In such cases, improved individual pit toilets might offer the most advantageous solution. Improved pit toilets, built on households' land, can use different functional and structural solutions. Generally the system of the improved individual pit toilet consists of a toilet seat compartment of Asian or European type, wastewater accumulation pit or septic tank and a pipe from the house to the pit. A toilet chamber can be installed inside the house, in which case the wastewater is removed to the septic tank or storage pit. It can be also placed in the area of the house's land plot, directly on the septic or storage pit, or adjacent to it. As a rule, a septic tank is planned when the house is equipped with a bathroom.

A septic tank is a waterproof tank, consisting of one or two divisions, made of plastic (prefabricated tanks), brick, concrete or reinforced concrete. Unless secondary treatment is provided (which is unusual for tanks serving individual houses and small institutional buildings), it must be followed by a drain field or soak away to allow the effluent to drain into the ground.

Depending on the type of soil, availability and levels of underground water resources, as well as on the position of the residential house, the storage pit can be made of concrete, rubble concrete, stone masonry, directly of soil, or modern materials. The storage pit can be draining or non-draining. There can be one or two, depending on the solution for removal of accumulated liquid and sludge. Where the groundwater is reasonably deep and/ or groundwater is not used for drinking, a draining pit will be the cheaper solution since completely waterproof pits (cess-pits) will require frequent emptying.

Large investment needs, little financing resources in Armenia

Investment needs for the sector are significant and dwarf recent levels of investment. Investments are required to achieve the following objectives:

- Achieve universal coverage with "improved" sanitation. It is important to note that universal coverage via sewer network extensions will not be achievable in the short to medium-term. In these circumstances, improved on-site sanitation standards need to be defined (and enforced) with strengthened faecal sludge management.

- Invest in new wastewater treatment facilities. Emphasis should be placed on investing in wastewater treatment in areas of pollution "hotspots" and via decentralised and local treatment solutions with low energy consumption or with solutions that emphasise energy recovery.

- Promote re-use of treated wastewater for irrigation and of (partially) treated faecal sludge from on-site sanitation.

- Accompanying reforms and "software measures" (such as demand promotion, support to planning at LSGB level, any institutional measures, etc.) will generate costs (sometimes referred to as "support costs) that will also need to be covered.

According to the preliminary assessment around EUR 2.6 billion investments will be required to meet Armenia's sanitation needs. The country's current economic situation and financial constraints mean that it will be necessary to stage such investments over time.

Strategic investment is required to avoid further deterioration of infrastructure, resulting in further increase of the financing gap. The focus should be on areas in which investment can lead to good return in terms of improved use of facilities, such as stemming further deterioration that would lead to a need for greater investment and the demonstration of new and improved approaches to sanitation provision and management. Change will have to be incremental and will involve a range of actions. Sensible approaches, however small, should be developed in order to create favourable conditions and attract financial resources to the sector.

The realistic approach: Defining targets for specific activities

Short-term, medium-term and long-term plans for the rehabilitation, improvement and development process of wastewater removal and treatment systems should be integrated, taking account of complete systems rather than individual components. This approach would allow achieving the ultimate objective of establishing a complete system in a staged way, through gradual increases in treatment capacity and expansion of sewerage coverage.

In the first instance, it is recommended to focus investments on "pollution hot spots", i.e. more vulnerable catchment areas such as Lake Sevan and/or those areas that receive a high polluting load. On this basis, the staging of investments could be done based on geographical areas. Complete systems, including appropriate treatment should first be built/rehabilitated in places that are environmentally sensitive and/or socially important (because for instance they are used for recreation). In areas that are less sensitive, it might be appropriate to consider sewerage followed by primary treatment in the first instance, particularly where this replaces direct discharges of untreated wastewater to water bodies. The key point here is to consider the effect that constructing new sewers will have on water quality. Moving away from dispersed to concentrated discharges (through the introduction of wastewater without treatment) may in some case create more harm than good. However, the pros and cons of these solutions will depend on the local situation.

There may be situations in which providing sewers moves pollution away from where people come into frequent contact with a water body. In such situations, there may be a case for providing sewerage without treatment in the first instance.

For example, if providing a sewer network to a particular community requires constructing of a 10 km long wastewater pipeline and a two-stage biological treatment plant, this would require EUR 100 million. If such sum is not available as a lump sum investment, then, depending on the available investment amount, the process can be launched in stages:

- Stage 1: Construct the sewer network in the most densely populated and the biggest polluter district of the settlement.

- Stage 2: Construct the first level of the wastewater treatment technological process, providing preliminary and primary treatment only (but including secondary treatment in environmentally sensitive areas). This should still have a positive impact on surface water quality.

- Stage 3: Depending on the size of the financial investments, gradually expand the sewerage network and provide full secondary biological treatment and sludge treatment at the wastewater treatment plant. In environmentally sensitive areas, tertiary treatment may be required.

However, providing some sort of treatment will always be better – both in absolute terms and politically. The challenge will be to decide priorities, bearing in mind the limited available budget. To do so, it will be necessary to model the impacts of discharges on rivers and lakes, focusing particularly on dissolved oxygen although other parameters could also be modelled. This can be done using relatively simple mathematical models – the challenge will be to collect the information to set up and prove the models.

An alternative to this "staged approach" would be a one-stage implementation of the entire programme. This approach would require large amounts of funds, however, which is not realistic in Armenia's conditions. In the absence of the required funds, it could only fund complete programmes in a few communities, leaving others in extremely poor condition. This approach would not be equitable.

Other than being realistic, a staged approach offers several advantages. It will:

- Achieve specific tangible results early in the programme, which will help to stimulate allocation of new investments.

- Include a greater number of communities, which will contribute to a balanced development of the settlements.

- Provide the opportunity to include specific sanitation sector responsibilities in the contracts with WSCs, providing the continuity and stability of improvement of sanitation systems even if the amounts planned under the allocated budget are small. In the case of a one-stage approach, even if some liabilities in WSCs for sanitation systems are included, the operator(s) will not be able to implement them because of the limited allocated budget and the large investments required under the wastewater improvement projects.

Improving Armenia's sanitation systems dictates a "Let's clean today as much as we can" approach, which requires adopting auxiliary reforms to the market structure in order to increase the efficiency and quality of sanitation service delivery, to the financing arrangements so as to generate additional funds for sanitation and to the legal framework.

The analysis has led us to the following investment estimate for the three stages identified:

- Short term (7-10 years): EUR 1012.9 thousand, including EUR 624 000 for the cities and EUR 389 000 for villages.

- Medium term (10-20 years): EUR 997.5 thousand, including EUR 631 000 for the cities and EUR 366 000 for the villages.

- Long term (20-30 years): EUR 589 000, including EUR 418 000 for the cities and 171 000 for the villages.

The estimates are based on the following assumptions:

- All the cities and part of the villages (with an average population up to 1.5 thousand) having centralised sewerage (the larger ones served by the WSCs and the smaller ones by LSGBs).

- Part of the villages (with an average population below 1.5 thousand) served by individual compact treatment plants or individual pit toilets.

The total estimated investment need stands at EUR 2.6 billion, with approximately EUR 1 billion needed in the next 7 to 10 years. This is a slightly lower investment estimates than presented during earlier stages of the study, as it is based on more significant reliance on alternative technologies described above. These costs have been estimated in Armenian Dram and converted to EUR at the rate of EUR 1 = AMD 530.

Operating costs associated with these new investments have been estimated at EUR 52 million annually, which would mainly need to be funded through tariffs. These estimates have been based on existing operating costs particularly in the larger towns. In villages, operating costs represent a lower percentage of capital costs, reflecting the fact that alternative technologies (with lower operating costs) will be used and also the fact that labour costs (which represent a large percentage of operating costs) are substantially lower in rural areas as compared to urban areas. These operating costs only include the costs of operating the systems and routine maintenance, and do not include the repayment costs of capital expenditure.

These values are indicative so as to provide an idea on the scale of the challenge. More detailed cost estimates will need to be prepared when the sanitation investment strategy is prepared.

Table 1.1. **Investment evaluations of wastewater treatment systems**

Settlement	Population, 1 000 persons	Capacity of WWTP m³/day	Unit Price of WWTP EUR 1 000	Number of WWTP, piece	Total investment mln EUR	Stage implementation		
						Short-term 7-10 y.	Mid-term 10-20 y.	Long-term 20-30 y.
1	2	3	4	5	6	7	8	9
Yerevan with centralised wastewater system	1 000.0	300.00	100 00	1	100.0	60.0	30.0	10.0
Gyumri with centralised wastewater system	250.0	55 00	37 000	1	37.0	20.0	14.0	3.0
Vanadzor with centralised wastewater system	130.0	30 00	28 000	1	28.0	18.0	8.0	2.0
Towns with centralised wastewater system	460.0 (av = 10.0)	88 00 (av = 2000)	4500	46	207.0	60.0	85.0	62.0
Total for cities					**372.0**	**158.0**	**137.0**	**77.0**
Villages with centralised wastewater system services by specialised Operators	1 000.0 (av = 2.0)	200 000 (av = 400)	350	500	175.0	60.0	60.0	55.0
Villages with centralised wastewater system, serviced by LSGB	312.0 (av = 1.5)	56 200 (av = 270)	250	208	52.0	20.0	20.0	12.0
Villages without centralised wastewater system, including:								
a) Planned to have individual compact treatment plants	12.0 (av = 0.48)	1 925 (av = 77)	3.5	1 700	6.0	3.0	2.0	1.0
b) With individual pit toilets for each household	72.0 (av = 0.48)	11 550 (av = 77)	1.0	18 000	18.0	8.5	7.0	2.5
Total for villages					**251.0**	**91.5**	**89.0**	**70.5**
Grand total					**623.0**	**249.5**	**226.0**	**147.5**

Note: **LSGB** – Local Self Government Body; **WWTP** – Wastewater Treatment Plant.

Source: Authors' own assessment.

Table 1.2. **Summary table of investments**

		Investment evaluation, mln EUR			Stage investment demand		
			including				
Settlement	Population, 1 000 persons	Total	ww removal system	WWTPs	Short-term 7-10 y.	Mid-term 10-20 y.	Long-term 20-30 y.
1	2	3	4	5	6	7	8
Yerevan with centralised wastewater system	1000.00	259.3	159.3	100.0	125.0	90.0	44.3
Gyumri with centralised wastewater system	250.0	185.8	148.8	37.0	85.0	64.0	36.8
Vanadzor with centralised wastewater system	130.0	117.3	89.3	28.0	58.0	43.0	16.3
Towns with centralised wastewater system	440.0 (av = 10.0)	900.5	693.5	207.0	310.0	335.0	255.5
Total for cities		**1462.8**	**1090.8**	**372.0**	**578.0**	**532.0**	**532.9**
Villages with centralised wastewater system services by specialised Operators	1000.0 (av = 10.0)	850.0	675.0	175.0	300.0	290.0	260.0
Villages with centralised wastewater system, serviced by LSGB	312.0 (av = 1.5)	259.5	207.5	52.0	100.0	90.0	69.5
Villages without centralised wastewater system, including:							
a) Planned to have individual compact treatment plants	12.0 (av = 0.48)	7.8	1.8	5.95	3.7	2.6	1.5
b) With individual pit toilets for each household	72.0 (av = 0.48)	21.8	3.8	18	10.3	8.0	3.5
Total for villages		**1 139**	**888.1**	**215.0**	**414.0**	**390.6**	**334.4**
Grand total		**2 602**	**1 979**	**623.0**	**992.0**	**992.6**	**687.3**

Note: **LSGB** – Local Self Government Body; **WWTP** – Wastewater Treatment Plant.

Source: Authors' own assessment.

Table 1.3. **Associated operating costs**

No.	Residential areas	Population	Required investments EUR mln	Annual operation costs EUR mln	Average annual wastewater flows mln m³/year
1	2	3	4	5	6
1	**Cities**				
	Yerevan with centralised wastewater system	1 000 000	259.3	19.80	110.0
	Gyumri with centralised wastewater system	250 000	185.8	4.44	25.6
	Vanadzor with centralised wastewater system	150 000	117.3	2.66	15.3
	46 towns with centralised wastewater system	460 000	900.5	7.02	40.3
Total for cities		1 860 000	**1 462.8**	**33.92**	**191.2**
2	500 villages with centralised wastewater system serviced by specialised Operators	1 000 000	850.0	13.56	65.7
3	208 villages with centralised wastewater system serviced by LSGB	312 000	259.5	3.93	18.2
4	175 villages without centralised wastewater system, including				
	a) Planned to have individual compact treatment plants (25 villages)	12 000	7.8	0.18	0.6
	b) With individual pit toilets for each household (150 villages)	73 000	21.8	0.65	2.6
Total for villages		1 397 000	**1 139.0**	**18.32**	**87.1**
Grand total		3 257 000	**2 601.8**	**52.24**	**278.3**

Note: **LSGB** – Local Self Government Body.

Source: Authors' own assessment.

References

AWSC/SAUR (2012), *Annual Reports 2010-2012.*

Armenian Marketing Association NGO, (2011), *Annual Survey of Social Impact of Water Supply and Sanitation services by Yerevan Water WSC.*

Government of Armenia (2012), *Rio +20: Republic of Armenia National Assessment Report*, Bavigh Printing House, Yerevan.

Government of Armenia (2010), *Armenia Millennium Development Goals, National Progress Report, 2005-2009*, Yerevan.

National Statistics Service of the RoA (2012a), *Preliminary Results of the 2011 Census,* Yerevan.

National Statistics Service of the RoA (2012b), *Statistical yearbook 2011,* Yerevan.

National Statistics Service of the RoA (2012c), *Environment and Natural Resources in the Republic of Armenia for 2011,* Yerevan.

National Statistics Service of the RoA (2012d), *Housing resources and public utility of the Republic of Armenia for 2011,* Yerevan.

Torres, A. (2013), *Armenia: Fostering the Long-Term Financial Viability and Sustainability of the Armenian Water and Sewerage Company*, Asian Development Bank, Working Paper Series, No. 4., Mandaluyong.

Chapter 2

Reforming market structure arrangements for sanitation in Armenia

This chapter describes the need for market reforms and discusses options available to the sanitation sector in Armenia. The chapter presents the fragmentation of the sanitation sector in Armenia and the impact this has on sector efficiency and impact upon public health and environmental performance as a key driver for reform. Five modes of service supply are explored with recommendations made on the implementation of the preferred model including the role of Government and incentives in the reform process.

Why market structure reforms needed and what are the options?

Current situation: A fragmented market

The organisation of the sanitation sector in Armenia is currently very fragmented, which results in service inefficiencies and creates risks for health and the environment.

The analysis mapped out how sanitation services are currently provided in Armenia, including by Water Service Companies (WSCs) and Local Government Bodies (LGBs). The market structure is complicated by the fact that water and sanitation services can be provided by different service providers.

On this basis, there were identified six modalities for the provision of water and sanitation services at household level in Armenia, as set out below:

- Mode 1: households get both water and sewerage services from a WSC. This is the most common mode of supply reaching an estimated 62% of the population, including the vast majority of the population residing in urban areas and a few rural territorial units.

- Mode 2: households get water services from a WSC and sewerage services from their LSGBs. This mode of supply is rare. According to the information available, 5 villages in Armavir and 8 villages in Shirak appear to be in this situation.

- Mode 3: households obtain both water and sewerage services from their LSGBs. This mode of supply is also uncommon. Nor Hachyn is a specific case here. This mode of supply is also present in Syuniq in the towns of Qajaran, Dastakert and in the town of Shamlukh on Lori.

- Mode 4: households obtain water from a WSC and rely on on-site sanitation solutions. This mode of supply concerns 9% of the population in all marzes apart from Yerevan, Aragastotn and Gegharquniq. In Koteyk, 32 villages are served by AWSC and rely on on-site sanitation.

- Mode 5: households get water from their local government and have on-site sanitation facilities. This mode of supply is the second most common after Mode 1 and is relevant for approximately 20% of the population distributed in almost half of territorial units in Armenia.

- Mode 6: households self-provide water (via local water service providers) and have on-site sanitation systems. This is the case for about 7% of the population. In Gegharquniq, 88 out of 93 villages self-provide water and sanitation services. This mode is also prominent in Lori.

Figure 2.1 shows how these different modalities were defined whereas Figure 2.2 represents their distribution frequency. This shows that whereas the majority of the population receives both water and sewerage services from the WSCs, the majority of territorial units (and about 20% of the population) fall under "Mode 5", which means that households get water services from their local government and have on-site sanitation facilities.

The need for reform

A window of opportunity is currently opened for reforming the structure of the Armenian water sector in greater depth that should consider in detail how to best organise sanitation service delivery.

Figure 2.1. **Modes of sanitation service provision in Armenia**

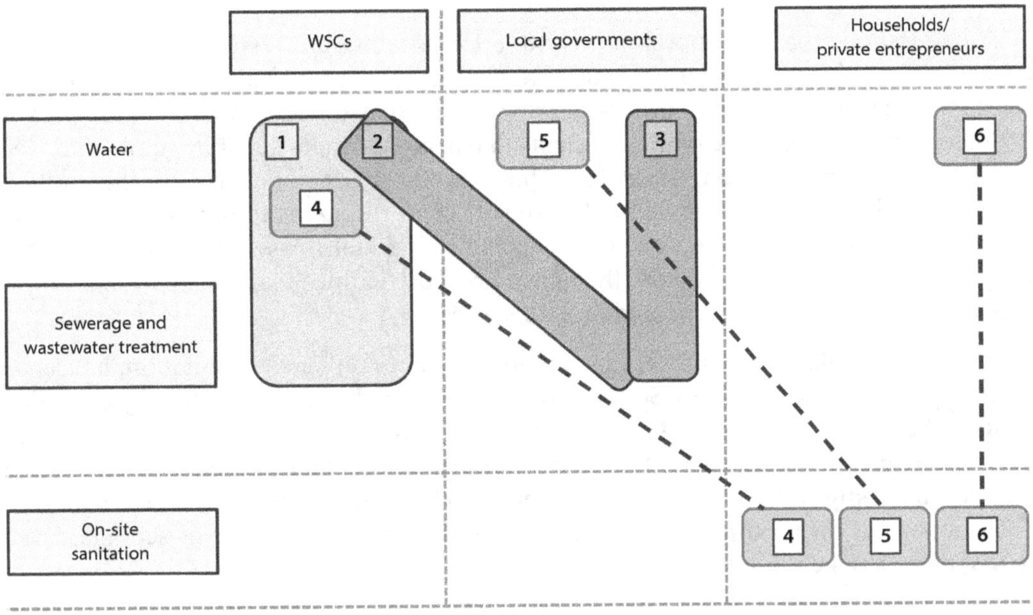

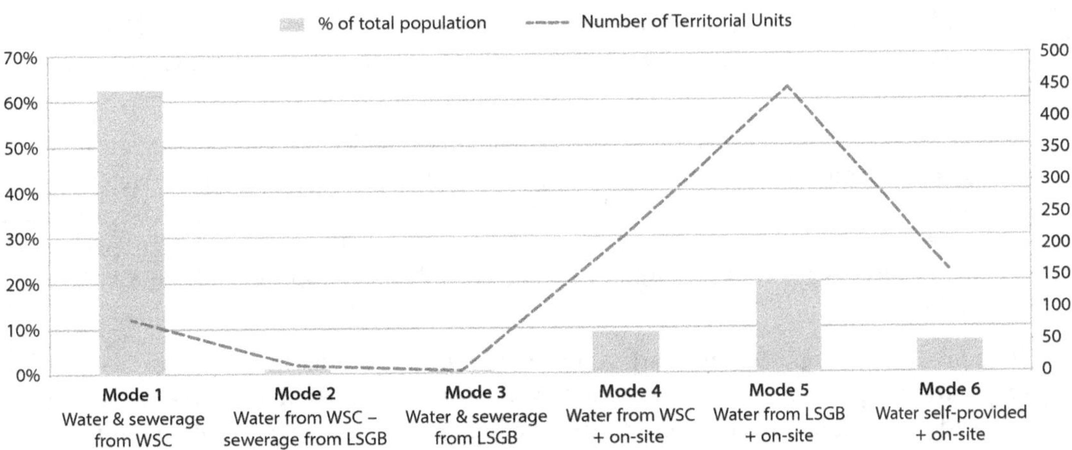

Source: Authors' own elaboration.

Figure 2.2. **Modes of sanitation service provision: frequency of distribution**

Note: **LSGB** – Local Self Government Body; **WSC** – Water and Sewerage Company.

Source: Authors' own elaboration.

All five WSCs (except Yerevan Djur) are currently running at a loss and are unable to generate funds to invest in the development of their services. Private sector participation contracts will end in 2015 and it is planned that new contracts will be signed to start in early 2016.

In addition, a study on the market structure of the Armenian water sector has recently been conducted, with funding from KfW, and has recommended in-depth changes to the water sector market structure in Armenia, including moving to a single water service provider for the whole country. However, the KfW study did not specifically examine the situation of sanitation services and the specific investment needs for the Armenian sanitation sector.

A key issue is that the approximately 840 LSGBs that are responsible for sanitation services do not have sufficient financial resources and technical capacities to ensure that appropriate sewerage services are provided or that on-site sanitation services are adequately supervised. Local governments have not formed separate units (i.e. legal entities) to manage sanitation services and they frequently do not charge for the sanitation services that they provide. They do not have sufficient resources to provide guidance and oversee the activities of entrepreneurs servicing individual households, including septic tank builders and emptiers. Finally, they have great difficulties to attract external funding for investment, from both public and private sources.

In the 823 territorial units where the population relies on on-site sanitation, households get no support from either the LSGBs or the WSCs, which means that they get no advice to guide them with the type of facilities to invest in or on scheduling regular emptying. There are no clearly defined standards for on-site sanitation and no means of enforcement to ensure that only improved facilities get built and are adequately serviced. In addition, LSGBs have not invested in sites for the safe emptying and handling of septage, i.e. the content of pit latrines and septic tanks.

Choosing the optimal market structure

Potential market structure reform options are usually considered alongside two main axes:

- Horizontal axis: over which area should sanitation services be provided? Sanitation services can be provided by entities that operate at different geographical scales; and

- Vertical axis: what range of services should be provided jointly? Sanitation services can be operated in an isolated manner, or combined with other services (water supply, district heating, storm water collection, solid waste collection, etc.). Also, different types of sanitation service can be provided by different entities. In particular, arrangements for on-site sanitation might be different from those for network-based sanitation.

The process for introducing market structure reforms can be top-down or bottom-up. In a ***top-down approach***, the market structure reforms are decided at central Government level based on pre-agreed geographical areas or service groups. In a ***bottom-up approach,*** gradual market structure changes are the result of decisions taken at the local level, with local governments deciding to join together to organise services based on local priorities. Such a bottom-up approach can either be the result of administrative aggregation (when local governments decide to form inter-communal structures for service delivery) or can be market-led (when the same private sector company wins service contracts for delivering services in several municipalities). Central government can facilitate bottom-up approaches by changing legislation to allow administrative aggregation and market-led responses and by providing incentives for local players to instigate bottom-up action.

The broad dimensions of market structure reforms translate into specific questions for Armenia:

- Should the existing structure of WSCs be maintained or could they operate more efficiently, generate more stable revenue flows and attract more investments into sanitation *(a)* if their geographic coverage or *(b)* if their vertical structure were modified (i.e. for example, by separating water and sewerage services or by grouping them with other services)?

- Should the current service areas of the WSCs be maintained or should they be encouraged/requested to provide sanitation services: *(a)* in all territorial units where they are already providing water services; *(b)* in all territorial units in a continuous geographical area (such as a marz or a river basin)?

- Should local self-governing bodies that are currently in charge of providing sanitation services retain full control over the selection of service provision arrangements, i.e. decide whether they should be overseeing the services themselves, contract service providers to deliver those services (such as a WSC) or be incentivised to join forces with other local self-governing bodies?

The answers to the above questions need to take account of contextual factors specific to Armenia, including: *(1)* a difficult geography as the country is very mountainous with limited potential for economies of scale; and *(2)* the legal context for inter-municipal co-operation and municipality enlargement and the dynamics between central and local governments.

Ongoing reforms affecting water and sanitation services market structure

A study funded by KfW and the government of Armenia on water sector management options has presented its preliminary recommendations in terms of optimal market structure. These options were formulated primarily for water services and with the perspective of introducing greater private sector participation into the sector.

The KfW study recommended greater aggregation of WSCs, with the formation of one, two or three WSCs and a gradual integration of municipalities not currently served by water services. The study considered different options for reforming the market, including having up to three operators for the country (as opposed to only one operator), i.e. one for Yerevan, one for AWSC as it currently exists and one or more for the existing regional companies, as the most interesting. Although the consultants recommended two WSCs as the most viable option, the government indicated a strong preference for forming a single WSC.

The study also pointed to other options, such as community water management and inter-community unions. These could be solutions for municipalities that might not be interested to join the regional operator. Alternatively, they might be selected as an interim solution.

The KfW study did not explicitly consider the situation of non-sewered municipalities, however. The recommendations contained in the present report therefore build upon the recommendations contained in the KfW study, but focus on sanitation and take into account the need to establish management arrangements for on-site sanitation systems.

Recommendations for market structure reforms

Based on these principles, the analysis suggests that the following options be adopted for reforming the sanitation sector market structure:

- LSGBs that currently receive sanitation services from a WSC (as in Mode 1 – i.e. 62% of the population) should continue to do so. The market structure reforms that would apply to them will be the same ones as for the water sector, which means that there might be one or two WSCs as a result of the reforms. There are no specific factors on the sanitation side, which means that the market structure for WSCs should be different for sanitation services vs. for water services.

- LSGBs that currently self-provide sanitation services (either through sewerage services or on-side sanitation services) should be given the opportunity to select the mode of supply that is most suitable for their own circumstances. It is recommended that an organic process be adopted, whereby the decision on the management of sanitation services rests with the LSGBs whereas the central government would provide support to LSGBs so that they can make the best decision possible.

Table 2.1 presents options for local governments for reforming the market structure in order to improve sanitation services. These options were discussed and have been accepted by stakeholders as being the main options offered to LSGBs for reforms.

The creation of multi-utility companies doesn't seem to be encouraged at this stage at local level on a large scale. This is due to the fact that WSCs are already managing substantial portions of the country: whether or not they want to deliver new services should be left to their own strategies rather than mandated from the top. In rural areas, the setting up of multi-service organisations could be distracting and counter-productive: it seems much more preferable to incite municipalities to go down the inter-municipal co-operation route.

Implementing the reforms: alternative process options

The supportive role of central government

Given that the ultimate decision on how to manage water and sanitation services rests with territorial units, a mix of "top-down" and "bottom-up" approaches is recommended to be adopted in order to stimulate sanitation market structure reforms. To avoid having to "force" a market structure change on LSGBs, financial incentives provided by the central government will be needed to induce the required changes while mitigating the risk of (political or social) resistance at local level.

In order to ensure that overall reform objectives are achieved, the central government should conduct a systematic audit of the water and sanitation conditions of the 930 territorial units. If this audit is not possible due to lack of resources, a series of in-depth case studies on the existing situation for territorial units in each of the six modes of supply should be commissioned so that suitable guidance can be provided to the LSGBs considering management options available to them in each of these six situations.

These case studies should be conducted in priority in "hot spot" areas, i.e. in vulnerable catchments such as Lake Sevan and/or those that are vulnerable because they receive a high polluting load (because they have high concentration of population and industry). In such hot spot areas, the aim would be to roughly assess the polluting loads from various sources, link polluting loads to supply modes and focus first on the areas and modes that are most polluting. The identification of actions in these areas could be used to show how systems can be improved and polluting impacts reduced.

The case studies below highlight real cases where market structure decisions will need to be taken in order to allow more efficient investment decisions. All of these case studies have been selected in areas where current pollution levels have been problematic, either around the Lake Sevan or in areas of tourism value.

Table 2.1. **Market structure key issues and potential options from LSGB'S point of view**

Mode of supply (Number of TUs and % population)	Rationale for market structure reforms	Potential options for LSGBs
Mode 1: water and sewerage from a WSC (86 TUs – 62% pop)	Need for horizontal aggregation of WSCs Need for vertical disaggregation?	Consolidation into one, two or three WSCs at national level (as proposed in the Water Sector Management Options study) TUs already receiving water and sewerage from an existing WSC should be strongly encouraged (via financial incentives and improved services) to remain in the service area of the new WSC (although they could elect to get out and form an ICU or a corporation) Letting separate BOT contracts for WWTP construction and operation could be considered as a way to attract private sector investment
Mode 2: water from a WSC and sewerage from their LSGBs (13 TUs – 1% pop)	Manage water and sewerage services jointly to generate economies of scope	TU to choose between two options: Transfer management of sewerage services to a WSC Join or participate in the creation of an ICU for sanitation
Mode 3: water and sewerage services from LSGBs (4 TUs – <1%)	Manage water and sewerage services jointly to generate economies of scope	TU to choose between three options: Transfer management of sewerage services to a WSC Join or participate in the creation of an ICU for sanitation Remain separate and establish a corporation
Mode 4: water from a WSC and on-site sanitation solutions (215 TUs – 9% pop)	Strengthen support to on-site sanitation	WSC given responsibilities to oversee on-site sanitation (provide technical support for construction and management of facilities, regular emptying services)
Mode 5: water from LSGB and on-site sanitation solutions (448 TUs – 20% pop)	Strengthen support to on-site sanitation	TU to choose between three options: Transfer management of water services to a WSC and WSC given responsibilities to oversee on-site sanitation Join or participate in the creation of an ICU for water and sanitation (ICU may invest in sewerage and WWTP project) Remain separate and establish a corporation, with responsibilities to oversee on-site sanitation
Mode 6: local water service providers or self-provision and on-site sanitation solutions (160 TUs – 7% pop)	Strengthen support to locally provided water schemes and on-site sanitation	TU to choose between two options: Join or participate in the creation of an ICU for water and sanitation services with responsibilities to oversee on-site sanitation Remain separate and organise community management for water services and overseeing on-site sanitation

Notes: 1. **BOT** – Build-Operate-Transfer; **ICU** – Intercommunity Unions; **LSGB** – Local Self Government Body; **TU** – Territorial Unit; **WSC** – Water and Sewerage Company; **WWTP** – Wastewater Treatment Plant.

2. In this table, the term Territorial Unit is used to refer to the geographical area that is managed by a single LSGB.

Source: Authors' own elaboration.

Case Study 1: Establishment and management of decentralised wastewater treatment system in Lake Sevan Basin area.

1. Brief description of current circumstances.

Lake Sevan is located in the Gegharkunik region and occupies an area of 1240 km². The lake is fed by 28 rivers, most of them important for fish production. One such river is Vardenik. It starts from Vardenis Mountains and flows through Vardenik village into Lake Sevan. Vardenik and Tsovinar villages are located on the Vardenik River bank.

Vardenik village is the second largest village in Armenia in population terms. The community has 10 700 inhabitants and 1 800 households. The population is mainly engaged in agriculture and cattle breeding. Vardenik village is located 40 km away from the region centre and 143 km away from Yerevan.

Water is supplied via a long transmission main from a groundwater source located about 25 km long to the south of the village. This scheme was built and is owned by local government. All households have internal house connections. 15% of the population receives a 24-hour water supply. The remaining population receives water by hourly schedule of 8-10 hours a day (5 hours in the morning and 3-5 hours in the evening). The water supply system of the village is in satisfactory condition. The residents do not have water meters and pay AMD 1 000 (EUR 1.83). The residents also pay if it is necessary to repair breakages in the water supply system.

About 30 % of the households are connected to the sewerage system, but there is no wastewater treatment plant. During the Soviet times, it was planned that the village's wastewater would be removed by ring collector and pumped to a wastewater treatment plant. However, the ring collector was not built and currently the wastewater is discharged into the Vardenik River, then into Lake Sevan, causing pollution of not only the river water, but also of the full basin and Lake Sevan.

The wastewater system has not been actively managed for many years. Currently there are frequent blockages and accidents, as a result of which wastewater flows into the settlement's area. This in turns increases the risk of epidemic diseases in the village, especially during the summer season.

The remaining households in the community have pit toilets (35%) or flush toilets (35%) from where wastewater goes into septic chambers installed at the border of their farmlands. Septic chambers are regularly emptied by cesspool emptiers but there are no facilities to receive septage. Cesspool emptiers may sell to farmers but it is likely that they discharge septage to rivers, causing severe pollution. These services are provided by private individuals or professional organisations and paid for by the residents.

The community also owns other wastewater systems, but the community does not have adequate human and technical resources to operate, maintain and develop them. In addition, improved financial systems will be required if they are to have the financial resources for effective operation and maintenance

Given the fact that in upper streams the Vardenis River's water is used for irrigation and power generation purposes, and the river's natural flow has significantly reduced, it can be concluded that a significant portion of the flow in the Vardenis River is wastewater. During dry periods, when natural flow is very low, the flow to Lake Sevan is likely to consist mainly of wastewater,

Tsovinar village is located on the left bank of the Vardenik River, at 1.5 km from Vardenik village. It has 5 450 inhabitants and 1 000 households. The population is mainly engaged in agriculture and gardening. The village is located 42 km from the region centre and 145 km away from Yerevan. The village is 2 km away from Lake Sevan.

Water supply to this community is sourced from underground springs by the local government. The drinking water pipeline starts from the natural springs at 30 km from the village, from where water is filled into 100 m^3 capacity storage reservoirs through two pipelines. 99% of the population receives a 24-hour water supply, and all households have internal house connections.

The village administration operates the water supply system of the village but they do not have adequate financial and technical resources and they operate mainly the two pipelines. The residents operate the internal network irregularly. The residents don't have water meters and pay AMD 1 000 (EUR 1.83) per year for water, according to the community council decision.

The community does not have a sewerage system. About 60% of the population uses pit toilets. The pit toilets are unimproved. Wastewater is mainly drained and since the village is located very near to Lake Sevan, the drained wastewater flows into the lake.

About 40% of the population has flush-toilets. The wastewater from bathrooms and toilets is filled into septic chambers installed at the border of their farmlands. Most chambers are not watertight and wastewater is drained into the ground. The toilets are not serviced by local government. Each resident operates his/her septic structure and from time to time pays an individual for its emptying.

2. *Improving sanitation services: recommended activities.*

In order to protect Vardenik River's ecosystem, reduce anthropogenic pressure upon Lake Sevan and improve of sanitation for Vardenik and Tsovinar communities, the following measures are required:

- Reconstruction and expansion of the wastewater system existing in Vardenik community.

  The existing wastewater system of Vardenik village needs reconstruction, as it has damaged segments because of not being operated for many years. It is necessary to restore approximately 600 segments of the sewerage network, which will cost about EUR 40 000. It is also proposed to extend the wastewater network, so that 50% more people can join the wastewater network. For this purpose it is needed to build a 2.3 km long new wastewater network (including 300 m collectors), which will cost EUR 200 000. Thus, for rehabilitation and expansion of Vardenik's wastewater system around EUR 240 000 will be required.

- Construction of wastewater system in Tsovinar village.

  It is proposed to fully sewer the densely populated part of Tsovinar village where 60% of the population lives. For this purpose it is necessary to build a wastewater network of 3.5 km length (of which 1.5 km collector to the wastewater treatment plant).

- Construction of a joint WWTP for treatment of Vardenik and Tsovinar communities' household wastewater.

It is proposed to construct a 2 000 m³/day capacity treatment plant at a equal distance from the two villages. Taking into account the space limitations, it is recommended to construct a combined (block) WWTP providing full biological treatment. This will be located close to the Vardenis River, which runs between the two villages. The approximate cost of the treatment plant will be around EUR 600 000 and the annual operation costs will be about EUR 42 000. The treated wastewater will be discharged into the Vardenis River, thereby contributing to replenishing the river's water resources. Some pumping from Tsovinar may be required because satellite images show that the eastern part of the village, furthest from the river, is lower than the western part.

3. Potential institutional models.

It is recommended to establish an inter-community union for the management and operation of water and wastewater systems of the two communities. Establishing the union will ease obtaining funds for the construction and reconstruction of the system. It may also help setting affordable tariffs for service provision as well as establish capacities for operation and maintenance of the system, including human capacity and technical equipment. An ICU would provide wider opportunities to expand the sewerage network to the communities.

To start this process, the following measures are necessary:

- Local governments and councils must formulate a decision to improve the sanitation system.

- The place for constructing the WWTP must be identified, including securing land and obtaining land category change.

- Establishment of the inter-community union by the two LSGBs and signing of a memorandum of understanding.

- Funding application.

4. Anticipated outcomes

- A decentralised household wastewater treatment and management system is created, operated by an inter-community union.

- Vardenik village's sanitary-hygienic condition is improved, the risk of epidemics reduced.

- The Vardenik River's and Lake Sevan water quality and sanitary-hygienic conditions in Lake Sevan Basin are improved.

- The Vardenik River is rehabilitated as a river of fishing importance.

- Anthropogenic pressure on Lake Sevan is reduced.

Case Study 2: Decentralised system for household wastewater treatment for Baghramyan and Myasnikyan villages.

1. Brief description of current circumstances.

Rural communities Baghramyan (1 054 inhabitants and 274 households) and Myasnikyan (4 507 inhabitants and 1 150 households) are located in the Armavir region at 65 km from Yerevan. The population is mainly engaged in fruit growing, viticulture, vegetable growing, and animal husbandry.

In both villages, the number of pensioners is big (35 %). They receive an average of AMD 26 000 (EUR 47.7) monthly pension; those receiving subsidy (25%) get a monthly average of AMD 24 600 (EUR 45.2). Unemployment is high, standing at 50 %.

The scarcity of irrigation water (and its inadequate quality) is a major problem for these communities, who have to leave large portions of land uncultivated. This problem is further exacerbated by uncertainties related to climate change and droughts in this area.

The water supply and sewerage systems are operated by Nor Akunq WSC. The company provides 24-hour water supply in both communities. Most households are connected to the central water supply system (93% in Baghramyan and 71% in Myasnikyan). Nor Akunq's maintenance activities are confined to breakages repair. The WSC is not responsible for the long-term development of the system.

Most inhabitants are connected to the sewerage system and equipped with flush toilets. Sanitation services are the responsibility of local self-government bodies, who are also the asset owners of the system.

During Soviet times, it was envisaged that the wastewater would be pumped through the collector to the Armavir treatment plant constructed at Metsamor. However, the construction of the system remained incomplete. Currently, Baghramyan village's household wastewater is removed to Myasnikyan through a 1 km-long collector and is then discharged into Talin canal. During the irrigation season, wastewater is mixed with irrigation water, resulting in poor qualitative indicators of lands in Baghramyan and the neighbouring villages. This situation exposes 10 500 people to acute intestinal infectious diseases.

Myasnikyan village administration often pays fines for discharging the wastewater into the irrigation canal. The Water User Association (WUA) often closes the outlet of the wastewater collector, resulting in wastewater discharge into the village areas. Conflicts arise not only between neighbouring villages, but also between the village administration and the WUA.

2. Improving sanitation services: recommended activities.

The proposed improvement to sanitation services in Baghramyan and Myasnikyan rural communities consist in the construction of a joint wastewater treatment plant for the two communities. The plant would be built in Myasnikyan community, at the end of the operating collector adjacent to the irrigation canal.

The priority of this intervention is to repair and rehabilitate the household wastewater collection, transportation and treatment systems. The emergency segments of the collector from Baghramyan to Myasnikyan (about 1 km in length), as well as the emergency segments of the collector passing through the area of Myasnikyan village (about 600 meters), should be restored. About EUR 200 000 are required for the rehabilitation of the emergency segments of the collector. The renovation and expansion of the internal sewerage network is not planned at this stage.

The treatment plant is planned in Myasnikyan village, in the vicinity of the irrigation canal. Taking into account the space limitations, it is proposed to construct a combined (block) WWTP with reinforced concrete structures. The approximate cost of the treatment plant will be EUR 250 000 and the annual operation costs will be about EUR 15 000.

At this stage, new connections to the operating system are not planned. To fully connect the two villages (and reach 100 % of customers), it will be necessary to rebuild and expand the internal sewerage network, which will cost EUR 300-350 million.

As a result of the treatment of household wastewater from the two communities, 10.52 l/s water amount will be generated. The treated wastewater can be used for irrigation purposes. It may be directed to Talin irrigation canal, where the treated wastewater water will be mixed with water for irrigation and will allow increasing available water during the irrigation season, which would not be subjected to seasonal fluctuations. As a result, this intervention will help mitigate droughts to some extent during the irrigation season.

Since the household wastewater of these settlements is currently mixed with the irrigation water without treatment, and the residents of these, as well as neighbouring villages irrigate their cultivated land with this water, they will not have objections against mixing the treated wastewater with irrigation water. The same can be stated about the WUA serving these communities: they will have additional irrigation water amount at the expense of the treated wastewater and will sell it to the residents. It could also be possible to envisage the option of selling the treated wastewater to the WUAs at a lower price, which can then be sold to farmers as irrigation water.

3. Potential institutional models.

Local governments are mandated to provide sanitation services, but they lack the human and technical resources required for the proper operation of the system. After rehabilitation of the system, local governments will give Nor Akunq WSC the responsibility to operate the rehabilitated system, as the WSC has the technical expertise to do so.

Baghramyan and Myasnikyan local governments have expressed their willingness to hand over the system for operation to Nor Akunq as of today. The WSC refuses to take over this function when the system is incomplete and in critical condition but they may consider doing so once the necessary investments in rehabilitation and expansion have been made.

The following actions are important for advancing this process, presented below not necessarily in sequential order:

- Decisions of the two communities' municipal councils to restore the system and build a treatment plant.

- Decision on land allocation for building of the treatment plant and land category change.

- Agreement signed between the Local Government and the Nor Akunq CJSC on operation of the system.

- Availability of funds. This will require formulating an application for funding, will a plan set out for all the above elements.

4. Anticipated outcomes.

- A decentralised household wastewater treatment and management system will be created, belonging to the communities and operated by Nor Akunq specialised company.

- 10.52 l/sec extra water amount for irrigation will be generated from the treated wastewater, which is constant and will be independent from weather conditions and climate change effects.

- Favourable conditions will be created for integrated management of water resources (irrigation water, treated household wastewater) available at the community level.

- Treated sludge will be generated, to be used as a cheap and good quality organic fertiliser (about 11 tons/year) to fertilise the land and obtain ecologically clean products (if treated adequately).

- Neighbouring communities' land degradation will be reduced (agricultural land contamination with sewage prevented) and their food security provided.

Case Study 3: Establishment of decentralised system for household wastewater treatment in recreation zone of the Dalar River.

1. Brief description of current circumstances.

The Dalar River is situated in Kotayk region and is the second major tributary the Hrazdan River (length: 14 km). With its favourable climatic conditions and picturesque nature, the river basin area is a twelve-month resort zone in Armenia. In its mid-stream, the river Dalar flows through Arzakan community. Arzakan village is located at 40 km distance from the capital, in the Aghveran resort zone and has 2950 residents and 700 households. The population is mostly engaged in agriculture and animal husbandry. The community has well-developed infrastructure; including school, kindergarten, musical school, culture centre. Arzakan is one of Armenia's wonderful places, due to its beautiful nature, refreshing air, deep forests and famous hot waters. It is a favourite destination for tourists. There are more than one thousand horticultural/cottage/farms and the "Aghveran" resort zone, with over 25 rest houses.

All residents have house connections to the water supply system, which is operated by the communities themselves. There are two systems for water supply. The first system is operated by the village administration: it sources water from Aghveran springs located at a distance of 15 km from the village and services approximately 70% of the village population. The water supply is carried out by time-schedule, the water supply duration being 12 hours daily. According to the decision of the village council, the residents supplied by this system pay AMD 100 (EUR 0.18) monthly. Although the village administration operates the system, it does not always have the required equipment and often has to rent these from specialised and private institutions. The internal network was built in the 1960s and is in worn-out state.

The second system is operated by the residents and services approximately 30% of the population. The subscribers of this system have twenty-four hour water supply. The residents do not pay fees, but in case of breakdowns, they have to pay for repair and spare parts.

Arzakan has no sewer network. About 80% of the population have flush toilets, which wastewater is discharged directly into the River Dalar without treatment. The river is used by 90% of the community population to irrigate farmlands.

Until the 1990s the wastewater from rest houses and health resorts built in the area of the upstream river Dalar was removed and treated at a treatment plant built with that purpose. Over time the plant has deteriorated and does not operate anymore.

Rest houses are currently polluting the area of the river Dalar and the resort zone. It has become urgent to create appropriate and comfortable sanitation facilities, to organise wastewater removal and treatment, to prevent irrigation with untreated water and adopt measures to protect the environmental conditions.

2. Improved sanitation services: recommended activities.

In order to protect the Dalar River's ecosystem, improving sanitary-hygienic conditions of the vacationers and local population, improving the quality of irrigation water, the following activities are recommended:

- Construction of a grouped WWTP for the rest houses of Aghveran resort zone.

  At present over 15 rest houses are operating in Aghveran resort zone, some of them are located close to each other, while the others are located at big distances from each other. It is proposed to construct a group WWTP for 5 rest houses, which are close to each other. For the other 10 houses, it is economically beneficial to have individual treatment plants, as their connection to group treatment plants will be quite expensive due to their location. This approach is efficient from the environmental point of view, since the treated wastewater from each rest house will be used to preserve the surrounding natural landscape.

  A 900 m long collector costing EUR 135 000 will need to be built for a wastewater system servicing the above-mentioned 5 rest houses. It is also planned to construct a WWTP on the bank of the Dalarik River. Considering the area's restriction, it is proposed to construct a combined WWTP with reinforced concrete structures. These could entail sedimentation tanks followed by trickling filters. The approximate cost of the treatment plant will be over EUR 140 000 with an estimated EUR 8 000 annual operation cost.

- Installation of improved toilets with waterproof pits in the informal resort zone.

  In the informal resort zone, it is planned to construct improved toilets with waterproof pits at the cost of EUR 2 000 each. In this area, the total cost of sanitation improvement will be EUR 200 000.

- Construction of wastewater system and a WWTP (in the future) in Arzakan village.

  In the future, it is planned to build a sewerage system and one treatment plant in Arzakan village, which will relieve the Hrazdan River and its Marmarik tributary from anthropogenic pressure. The construction of the sewerage system for the village (up to 80% connection of residents to the sewerage system) will require the construction of a 4 km long internal network and a collector at an approximate cost of EUR 500 000. The treatment plant will be constructed out of Arzakan village, on the left side of Arzakan-Teghenik road, on the right bank of the Hrazdan River, between the road and the river. Considering the area's restriction, it is proposed to construct a combined (block) WWTP with reinforced concrete structures. The approximate cost of the treatment plant will be over EUR 180 000 with an annual operation cost of EUR 10 000. The treated wastewater will be discharged into different parts of the Dalarik River and also the Hrazdan River, increasing the river water resources and enabling the irrigation of larger agricultural areas. However, it is important to note that allowing different discharge points would generate additional costs, as it would require a system of pipes and valves. Alternatively, all flows could be discharged in the river in one single point.

3. Potential institutional models.

Arzakan community's water supply system is the property of LSGB and is operated by them. To improve service management, it is advised to establish a corporate management system with the participation of the LSGB and the rest houses. The management of this system should be delegated to a specialised organisation on a contractual basis. Such corporate management will allow reducing the operation costs, by for example, running the system with a minimum staff.

The LSGB will act as an initiator and organise the construction and operation of the three systems in the Dalar river basin. A key objective for the LSGB could be to reduce the wastewater removal and treatment cost for the village's residents, by applying a surcharge for the rest houses' vacationers.

The system's operator will also be mandated to service the improved facilities in the informal resort zones and for the 20% of Arzakan village population using pit toilets.

To reduce operating costs of the treatment plants, the 10 rest houses in the resort zone (excluded from the grouped WWTP) could be involved in the management of their individual WWTP, rather than contracting organisations, as the latter could lead to price increases.

The following is needed in order to implement this process:

- preliminary agreement between LSGBs and the rest houses
- land allotment and soil category modification for the construction of the treatment plants
- establishment of a corporation with the participation of the LSGB and the resort houses
- acquisition of funds.

4. Anticipated outcomes.

The following outcomes are expected:

- Established household wastewater removal, treatment and management through a decentralised system, belonging to the community and operated by it or by other specialised organisation on a contractual basis.
- Improved water quality in the rivers Dalar and Hrazdan and improved sanitary-hygienic conditions of the river basins.
- Prevention of epidemic outbursts and favourable conditions established for the vacationers in the informal resort zone.
- Improved irrigation water quality in the Arzakan community.

- Reduced degradation of community lands (prevented pollution of agricultural lands with untreated wastewater) and improved food security for the population.

The **central government** should also support the establishment of the policy framework that can enable LSGBs to select the best sanitation option. Such framework should include:

1. Introducing incentives or obligations for WSCs to serve new territorial units with sewerage services or to supervise the delivery of on-site sanitation services.

2. Approaches to foster inter-municipal co-operation for wastewater projects (and other services).

3. Support systems for local governments, to enable them to plan sanitation services, apply for funding for investment projects (in sewerage or sewage treatment facilities) and supervise on-site sanitation services.

The following sections examine in turn these three dimensions of a supportive policy framework for developing sanitation services.

The incorporation of new territorial units into the service areas of WSCs could be incentivised via introducing coverage extension obligations in the new contracts with the WSCs (likely to be either one or two WSCs following market structure reforms, as outlined above). If the precise list of territorial units to be incorporated is not clear, a general clause should be introduced in their contracts to define a process for incorporation of new territorial units into the perimeter of the WSCs and how the financial consequences of this incorporation will be dealt with. Such incorporation is recommended to be made as income-neutral as possible through the provision of financial incentives to WSCs to incorporate these territorial units. These could include public funding for works to be carried out prior to incorporation to be provided by the central government.

Fostering inter-municipal co-operation

Forming Intercommunity Unions (ICUs) for sanitation services would be most relevant for specific investment projects, such as the construction and subsequent operation of a wastewater treatment plant or a faecal sludge treatment plant. ICUs could also be formed in areas of specific environmental value. For example, an ICU could be established to handle sanitation services (and potentially a range of other services as well, including solid waste management services) in the area of the Lake Sevan, the largest freshwater resource in the country. Case study 1 above shows what this might mean in practice. It proposes that two villages could cooperate, forming an ICU, to build and manage a new wastewater treatment plant that would reduce polluting discharges to Lake Sevan.

Existing examples of ICUs in Armenia are relatively rare, however, and most of them have formed with substantial support from international organisations. In order to support their creation for sanitation investments, it is necessary to further develop the legal framework for inter-community co-operation, as well as providing financial incentives for the formation of such ICUs for sanitation.

Financial incentives will need to be provided to LSGBs to form ICUs, given their poor financing capabilities. International experience, including in Europe, has shown that inter municipal co-operation (IMC) is supported using central government transfers, whether through ear-marked grants or more general grants, especially to initiate the formation of these associations. In Italy for example, various state mechanisms have supported the establishment of inter-municipal groupings, including special funds dedicated to finance 15% of the initial costs.

Joint inter-municipal projects could be encouraged by imposing specific conditions to grant applications that are submitted to the central government. Several programmes supported by the EU (see for example, the Instrument for Pre-Accession or Cohesion Fund) and other international donors operate in this way, by either setting up a minimal threshold for the project size (which is set at a high level, making it hard for smaller municipalities to apply and thereby giving them an incentive to associate) or positively discriminating applications from more than one municipality.

The planned establishment of the Regional Development Fund in Armenia could incentivise the formation of ICUs. The recent EU-funded report on the Regional Development Policy for Armenia recommends that: "the RDF focuses primarily on larger-scale regional projects (at least inter-municipal)" (ECORYS, 2014). One option would be to arrange the RDF scoring system in a way that positively discriminates in favour of project proposals submitted by more than one municipality. Such an initiative would be justified where joint sanitation projects would be more effective and provide better value for money. The assessment of grant applications could also take account of factors such as the number of users. In this case, smaller municipalities would be incentivised to find ways to co-operate with other local governments.

In addition, companies set up under ICUs for sanitation projects could also be assisted with tax "holidays" and deductions. This is well justified from the public finance perspective given that adequate sanitation, at least in part, is a public good. Such tax breaks could be applied to both corporate income tax and import duties for items such as wastewater treatment equipment and prefabricated septic tanks.

A major task of the Government is to provide legal and technical assistance to municipalities for forming Intercommunity Unions. This can be done by the Ministry of Territorial Administration (MTA)/SCWS or at marz level. Such assistance supposes that government staff is trained to provide guidance and appropriate technical support. The Government should also support information sharing, research studies, seminars, and promotion campaigns.

One efficient incentive would be to provide financial and technical support for the initial feasibility studies for setting up ICUs. A special funding line could be initiated at the SCWS for such studies, which should be administered in a competitive manner.

Fostering the establishment of ICUs will not be easy, however. The Government, with IFI support, should support several carefully chosen ICU pilots for sanitation, in order to demonstrate the accrued benefits. Besides the lack of a national tradition and other obstacles hindering such co-operation, there are many inherent challenges that have to be taken into consideration. The biggest challenge will be to overcome the competition of the participating municipalities against each other. The selection of pilot projects should favour municipalities where there is a need for joint investments and common challenges are perceived by stakeholders.

Rural-urban partnerships could be incentivised as special kinds of ICU. The improved co-ordination between investments in urban and rural areas can contribute to prevent inefficiencies caused by duplication of infrastructure and institutional arrangements and can ensure that there are no gaps in provision, particularly in peri-urban areas. This is especially important when rural population is declining, which leads to a diminished infrastructure utilisation and thus to higher per-capita costs for households.

Box 2.1. **Elements needed to trigger an Intercommunity Unions (ICU)**

Usually, the need to perform a certain service or to build some infrastructure jointly brings municipal leadership to establishing an Inter-Community Union. There must be a generally perceived feeling that the existing situation needs to be improved. If citizens or municipalities are not concerned, they will not want to embark on a complex venture such as setting up an ICU. It might therefore be a good idea to carry out a customer satisfaction survey to determine if there is sufficient demand for change. This survey could be accompanied, where possible, by a baseline research project on the way municipalities currently perform in delivering the targeted services. This will also enable any progress under the ICU to be properly assessed.

Champions of inter-communal co-operation should seek to identify untapped potential that co-operation with neighbouring municipalities could help to exploit. Acknowledging problems will remain unproductive without someone who can transform existing dissatisfaction (e.g. a polluted river) into a vision and propose inter-municipal co-operation as the way forward. Champions must also consider whether similar problems exist in bordering municipalities and if dissatisfaction is spread there too, and whether there are opportunities that might benefit several municipalities if exploited.

Interested municipalities should start a process of getting a range of people on side to discuss the possibility of establishing an ICU as a tool to address drawbacks in local public service delivery or to develop needed infrastructure. Such discussion should include elected representatives, managers and staff, local businesses, NGOs, and citizens in general.

Potential partner municipalities should be brought together to ascertain which municipalities would be interested in joining forces to meet common challenges and start identifying possible areas where co-operation is likely to be viable.

Source: COE/UNDP/OSI-LGI (2010), *Toolkit Manual: Inter-municipal Co-operation.*

Establish support systems for local governments

A review of international experiences highlighted three potential approaches for supporting municipalities in formulating their plans for sanitation:

- Option A – Establish a publicly-funded organisation that could channel technical expertise and funding to municipalities for improvement of sanitation (and water) services – potentially combined with proposed Armenia National Sanitation Fund.

- Option B – Introduce obligations for WSCs to provide technical support to LSGBs (this could potentially be done through a fee-paying service).

- Option C – Foster the establishment of an association of municipalities that is specifically working on sanitation issues (or potentially water and sanitation).

Additional details are provided on each of these options below.

Option A – Establish a publicly-funded organisation to channel technical expertise and funding

A publicly-funded organisation could be set-up with a specific remit to channel technical expertise and funding to municipalities for improvement of sanitation (and water) services. The establishment and operation of such an organisation would require dedicated funding, which would most likely need to come from an external funder, at least to cover initial set-up costs.

Setting up this type of organisation would have clear advantages: it would provide a clear interlocutor for LSGBs looking to develop their sanitation services and would serve as a national repository of expertise, with respect to the promotion of sanitation as well as technologies. This organisation could also issue norms and standards relative to on-site sanitation that would guide its adoption and supervision by LSGBs.

This type of reform can set the stage for what is sometimes referred to as "light regionalisation", which involves creating a regional institution that could be "sub-contracted" some tasks in both water and sanitation: prepare capital investment projects; tariffs studies, advice on technical, legal, financial and organisational questions, water loss analysis, emergency water supply service maintenance services, education and training etc.

This organisation could potentially house a funding mechanism such as the proposed Armenian National Sanitation Fund, although an arms' length relationship should preferably be maintained between departments to avoid conflicts of interest. For example, the same individuals should not be in charge of providing support to LSGBs for the preparation of their sanitation plans and simultaneously be responsible for selecting which LSGBs can receive funding on the basis of these sanitation plans.

Option B – Introduce obligations for WSCs to provide technical support to LSGBs

If the creation of a dedicated organisation is not possible, it might be possible to transfer some technical support functions to the WSCs, so that they could support even the LSGBs that are not in their service areas with specific technical tasks, such as siting and designing facilities or providing technical assistance for their ongoing management. The more established WSCs (including Yerevan Djur and AWSC) are the best repository of sector knowledge at present, particularly from a technical point of view, and could be requested to provide technical assistance to LSGBs (potentially at a fee), through contractual obligations. However, they may resist the extension of their functions in geographical areas where they are not currently operating or place a low priority on these activities.

In order to ensure WSC's co-operation, they should receive appropriate incentives to engage in these activities: an appropriate remuneration (through a fee) should first be provided. This could be per service provided or in the form of ongoing service contract. The latter form would be preferable in order to ensure their long-term co-operation and provide them with some element of cost-sharing across small towns where they operate.

Option C – Foster the establishment of an association of municipalities that is specifically working on sanitation issues (or potentially water and sanitation)

Alternatively (or preferably in parallel), the establishment of an association of municipalities to work specifically on (water) and sanitation issues should be considered. Such an association would represent the interests of local governments in the national debate, including when a sanitation strategy is being defined. This would also facilitate exchanges of experiences with respect to management models and technologies. In order to be truly representative, however, this association should be created and supported by the LSGBs themselves: it would be more difficult to create such an association purely as a result of a central government intervention.

These three options are complementary (i.e. not mutually exclusive) and could be pursued simultaneously in order to provide as much support to LSGBs as possible when they need to select the most appropriate way to deliver sanitation services.

Provided funding was available, it is strongly recommended the establishment of a dedicated institution in charge of supporting LSGBs for supervising and/or providing sanitation services (i.e. Option A). If this option is retained, it should form part of the national sanitation strategy. This should be followed by the drafting of an organisational structure and business plan (including staffing and financing plans). Numerous examples of this kind of structures exist that can provide a good reference point, including in the electricity sector.

References

COE/UNDP/OSI-LGI (2010), *Toolkit Manual: Inter-municipal Co-operation*

Sustainable Sanitation Alliance (2009), *Case study of SuSanA project: UDD toilets in rural school*, Yerevan.

Tumanyan, D. (eds.) (2012) *Local Self-Government Reforms in Armenia: 2011*, Book 4, Communities Finance Officers Association of Armenia, Noyan Tapan, Yerevan.

UNECE (2010), *Lessons Learned from the Implementation of the Armenian NPD on IWRM*, United Nations Economic Commission for Europe, Geneva.

Urban Foundation for Sustainable Development (2011), *The role of Central Government in Facilitating The Development of Decentralised Water Supply and Sanitation Services: The Case of Armenia.*

USAID Armenia/Counterpart International (2011), *Expanding Opportunities for Financing Local Government Service Delivery and Infrastructure through Public-Private Partnerships*, Civil Society and Local Government Support Programme, CSLGSP.

Veolia Water/Yerevan Water WSC (2012), *Annual reports 2010-2012.*

World Bank (2011), *Republic of Armenia: Water Sector Note*, Sustainable Development Department Europe and Central Asia Region, Report No. 61317-AM.

Chapter 3

Reforming financial arrangements for sanitation in Armenia

This chapter presents the current situation with regard to financing of the sanitation sector in Armenia. The shortfall in available funds from existing traditional sources such as tariffs is presented with the chapter considering options for generating additional revenues from tariffs. The current public funds available for sanitation are discussed and options are considered for increasing funds through reform of existing funds or creation of new funds.

Evaluation of the current situation

Financing can come from several sources to cover the financing needs of the sector: tariffs, domestic taxes, international transfers, and private repayable financing. None of these sources are utilised adequately at the moment to address sanitation challenges. Tariffs are at below cost-recovery levels, there is very limited funding from the central and local governments and international funding is going mainly towards improving water supply (except the recent project funding a few WWTPs) and virtually non-existent private funding.

The Sections below discuss the proposed improvements to some of these funding channels. These were discussed during the workshop in Yerevan on 1 April. 2014. The current report incorporates the feedback received

Tariffs and charges

Tariffs should be a main source of funding for the sector, even if there is a need for additional public funding to finance new investments. However, the current level and structure of tariffs for all types of sanitation services are inadequate and do not enable recovering operating costs of services.

Table 3.1 provides options for reforming tariffs in order to increase revenues.

Public funds for sanitation

Central government

Public funds for sanitation are very limited. The government, in charge of capital expenditure in the existing PPP projects, sources its funds from taxes and loans from IFIs. However, it currently has limited borrowing capacity. It can provide subventions to local governments, but the procedure for obtaining subventions for sanitation projects is currently cumbersome, which reduces local governments' ability to obtain funds.

Local governments

Local governments have few revenue sources, as decentralisation is not sufficiently advanced. They have little to no access to loans from commercial banks, IFIs or the government, due to excessive fragmentation and the lack of strong inter-municipal co-operation. Fragmentation also acts as a deterrent to the introduction of private sector participation for the provision of sanitation services.

In areas covered by the five WSCs, local governments could contribute to financing sanitation services if these companies were making a profit. However, this is predominantly not the case at present. In areas covered by Nor Akunq, Lori and Shirak WSCs, where local governments hold 49% of the companies, as well as in some areas covered by AWSC where local governments have provided only very limited co-funding for the connection of some districts to sewerage. The situation is similar in areas covered by Yerevan Djur, where Yerevan Municipality owns 100% of the shares of the company.

In areas where the sewerage networks are not managed by the five WSCs, local governments rely on small grant funding from international donor agencies (e.g. GIZ, USAID) and from the Armenian Social Investment Fund (ASIF) for capex. Opex is grossly underfunded through tariffs/charges. However, many local governments do not actually charge for their services. Nor Hachyn is the only municipality, which has established a

Table 3.1. **Alternative options for generating additional revenues from tariffs**

Diagnostic	Options to consider
Sewerage services – Domestic users	
• Tariffs for sewerage and sewage treatment services applied by WSCs do not fully cover operations and maintenance costs • Tariffs for sewerage services applied by WSCs, including wastewater treatment where such treatment is in place, represent between 9 and 19% of the combined water and wastewater tariffs (depending on the WSC). This might partly be explained by the total absence of wastewater treatment in many parts of the country. • In areas not covered by WSCs, it was estimated that only 20% of communities collect user charges for water supply and wastewater services.	• Increase wastewater tariffs closer to cost-recovery levels • Modify tariff structure, especially to alleviate the social impact of tariff increase: • Introduce two-part tariffs, with one "lifeline" tariff below O&M recovery costs for consumption below a certain volume of consumption and a higher tariff for all consumption above this threshold. The higher tariff should cover at least the operating and maintenance costs plus a margin to compensate for the subsidy provided to lifeline tariff consumers. • Introduce a "sanitation extension tax" to raise funds from customers currently connected to the sewerage network and cross-subsidise those who are not currently connected. In France, a similar tax exists but is applied to raise funds to rehabilitate existing sewerage networks ("*redevance pour modernisation des réseaux de collecte*").
Sewerage services – Non-domestic users	
• There are no specific tariffs for non-domestic/industrial users • There are no differentiated tariffs to reflect the pollution load that industrial users are discharging into the sewerage system, even though high loads would usually generate higher treatment costs • Environmental fees and fines that are currently levied by the State Environmental Inspectorate (SEI) for discharges of harmful substances into water bodies are currently set at very low levels	• Introduce differentiated tariffs for non-domestic (and particularly industrial) users, with reasonable level of cross-subsidies with household tariffs • Introduce "extra strength" tariffs to reflect the pollution load that industrial users are discharging into the sewerage system • Introduce incentives or penalties to ensure that industrial users connect to sewerage networks
Self-provision – Service users	
• Affordability constraints and lack of technical knowledge mean that at least 68% of rural households (in particular) are investing in unimproved sanitation solutions	• Investigate the motivations for household investments into on-site sanitation and design interventions to promote household investments into improved sanitation solutions • Facilitate access to finance: establish linkages with microfinance institutions so that the latter start offering microfinance products for sanitation investment by households or small-scale businesses • Organise the faecal sludge management sector and foster the development of scheduled emptying services for on-site sanitation

Source: Authors' own elaboration.

company for the management of sanitation services. Where there is no sewerage system, local governments do not provide financing for sanitation, despite their mandate to ensure adequate sanitation.

Environmental fees and fines

Government estimates indicate that compensations from the current level of nature use and environmental payments are 32-40 times lower than the actual damage caused. Furthermore, environmental fees paid by polluting organisations are not ring-fenced to provide funds for implementing environmental or health related projects in the impacted communities.

Increasing funds through existing and prospective funds

There are several funds that communities can approach to obtain funding for sanitation. However, these funds generally focus on water supply and tend to have specific selection criteria, generally prioritising the poorest locations. Communities that do not fall in this category may not be able to obtain funds under current selection criteria.

Considering the scale of the investment needs of the sanitation sector, existing (or planned) funds should explicitly include sanitation as a priority sector. The development of a national strategy for sanitation should help to align funding criteria with sectorial policies.

The main existing funds, which communities could potentially solicit funding from are the Armenian Social Investment Fund (ASIF), Hayastan All-Armenian Fund and the Renewable Resources and Energy Efficiency Fund (R2E2). In addition, funds for sanitation could be channelled in the near future via the planned Regional Development Fund (RDF) and the Eastern Europe Energy Efficiency and Environment Partnership (E5P). Table 3.1 provides a brief overview of the type of funding that these funding mechanisms could provide.

The Armenian Social Investment Fund (ASIF)

ASIF provides support for infrastructure rehabilitation. In March 2014, the GoA decided that ASIF will be transformed to become the Regional Development Fund (RDF), but no further details were available at the time of writing. Grant money channelled through the Fund goes to local governments, community organisations and NGOs to rehabilitate basic infrastructure. The Fund's portfolio of "micro projects" comprises the rehabilitation of about 893 facilities, including small-scale school rehabilitations (49%), potable water projects (19%) and community and cultural houses (12%).[1] In its current funding cycle (ASIF III), the Fund micro project typology includes:

- social infrastructure and goods

- economic infrastructure, including renovation, rehabilitation and construction of potable water systems limited to those based on small wells and surface springs, small-scale local level irrigation systems, including reservoirs which are not connected to trans-boundary waterways

- sanitation and environmental infrastructure, including renovation, rehabilitation and construction of sewerage systems (only upon the condition of having the system connected to the main sewerage network or the presence of a wastewater treatment plant downstream) and storm water channels and drains.

ASIF adopts a demand-driven approach and requires direct community involvement in the definition and identification of the micro project, along with supervision of the works.

Local government is represented in any implementing agency that carries out the actual micro projects, and will be responsible for maintenance after project completion.

ASIF activity in each region starts from mapping and ranking communities (urban and rural) so as to define the list of the neediest communities. Following this mapping exercise, the communities are classified into 3 clusters: Cluster A – Most vulnerable, Cluster B – Moderately Vulnerable, Cluster C – Least vulnerable. The list of potential applicants is compiled in the first instance from the most vulnerable communities in Cluster A. If there is a shortfall in the number of applications from cluster a, applications is sought from Cluster B. Thereafter, community meetings are organised in the selected communities to identify priority community works projects in a participatory setting. As a rule, each urban community may submit an application limited to one micro project. A reservation is made for Yerevan, Gyumri and Vanadzor. Each of 12 communities of Yerevan and cities Gyumri and Vanadzor may submit applications limited to two micro projects. Additionally the Department of Education of the Yerevan municipality submits the list of potential applicant schools in conformity with the funds allocated for Yerevan.

IDA funding has been the main source of funding for ASIF, reaching USD 33.2 million so far. In addition, according to ASIF procedures, for a micro project to be approved, the community has to contribute up to 5% of the estimated micro project cost. Richer communities are encouraged to pay higher community contribution. These contributions can be *(a)* monetary, e.g. budget allocation by the local authorities, small amounts raised from all the members of the community, contributions from alternate sources; and *(b)* non-monetary, e.g. labour contribution, construction materials, etc.

ASIF also supports capacity building efforts focused specifically on the provision of basic training in financial management, budgeting, accounting and asset management. The training benefits mayors, finance officers, accountants, and village council members and is limited to those small and medium-size communities where the ASIF has implemented projects.

ASIF undertakes outreach activities to disseminate information about the Fund among communities, local institutions and government. This activity also aims at increasing communities' capacity in micro project identification, prioritisation and proposal formulation.

The Hayastan All-Armenian Fund

The Hayastan All-Armenian Fund is an institution whose mission is to unite Armenians and to help establish sustainable development in Armenia and Artsakh. The Fund implements its projects through a global network of 25 affiliates. The funds' financial resources are obtained through a variety of fundraising activities. As of now, the total cost of the projects that it has supported in Armenia and Artsakh stands at more than USD 235.8 million.

The Fund's activities include the construction or renovation of roads, schools, kindergartens, hospitals, and water and gas networks, as well as assistance to socially vulnerable groups.[2] Each year, Hayastan All Armenian Fund's Board of Trustees determines the overall course of the Fund's activities for the year. This overall direction is based on the urgency and the strategic importance of the issues at hand. The Fund also undertakes special initiatives: projects that cover a whole spectrum of development and social assistance and cultural projects based on the wish of an individual benefactor or a community.

The Hayastan All-Armenian Fund has a programme dedicated to revitalising border villages. The Hayastan All Armenian Fund Rural Development Programme sees the solution to social and economic problems of border villages in restoring core infrastructure as well as stimulating the economic activity in the beneficiary villages. As first beneficiaries of the Rural Development Programme, the Fund chose six border villages in Tavush region: Aknaghbyur, Azatamut, Ditavan, Lusadzor, Lusahovit and Khashtarak. A number of key infrastructure projects are currently in progress (none related to sanitation so far). The Fund is also striving to reach out to the other border communities of Armenia with projects currently pending for villages in Lori and Syunik regions.

The Renewable Resources and Energy Efficiency Fund (R2E2)

The R2E2 was established by the Government as an independent NGO, with the main objectives to facilitate investments in the energy sector. R2E2 implements a comprehensive set of activities related to energy efficiency and renewable energy, supporting project developers, investors, banks, condominiums, researchers and others.

R2E2 supports the commercialisation of energy projects, typically small-scale ones, and finances them through banks and other lending institutions. The Fund strives to establish business partnerships and working relations between a wide range of actors in the energy sector: *(a)* the central government (including the MENR, the PSRC, the ADA and the Central Bank), *(b)* international organisations (e.g. the World Bank, the EBRD, EU), *(c)* public, international and private companies, including gas and electricity companies, *(d)* commercial banks, *(e)* NGOs, and *(f)* research institutions.

R2E2 has implemented a World Bank-funded project, which involved one component related to sanitation, for energy from the Yerevan WWTP. The overall objective of this project was to demonstrate how financing for renewable energy resources could be mobilised from IFIs and the private sector to stimulate the development of low carbon energy in the country. The Yerevan energy component included its modernisation with equipment for anaerobic treatment and aims to increase volume of wastewater treated by 125 million gallon per day by 2025.

R2E2 could make funding available for sanitation investments based on the potential for developing biogas usage.

The Regional Development Fund (RDF)

The government plans to establish the RDF as part of the implementation of its "Strategy for the Balanced Development of the Regions" (June 2011). The objectives of this Fund are: *(1)* to implement projects aimed at socio-economic development of the regional level using PPPs, and support to the projects implemented by the private sector; *(2)* to build the financial and institutional capacities of local communities to enable them to provide better services in solid waste management, street lighting, communal services, etc. This will include credit rating of the local governments and issuance of municipal bonds (with state guarantees if deemed necessary), soft loans with variable interest rates, depending on the geographical and geopolitical position of the communities; *(3)* to foster IMC through positive discrimination of the projects presented by more than one local governments; and *(4)* to provide investment capital to projects of national significance.

The GoA proposes to allocate 1% of the state budget annually to the RDF. Additional financial sources would include international loans and grants and contributions by the local governments. The government plans that 50% of the Fund's resources will be used to finance PPP projects, while 30% will be earmarked for infrastructure, 10% will be reserved for innovative projects targeting socio-economic development and the remaining 10% for loans to the local governments.

It is suggested that the RDF would use all of the following financing instruments: subsidies (soft loans and grants), bank guarantees, capital investment projects, and support to private sector projects through supporting infrastructure, and transfer of the state property to the communities into their own property or as management.

In regards to transforming ASIF into the RDF, two areas remain unclear at present: *(a)* the mode of operation of the future RDF; and *(b)* what features of the current ASIF will be preserved in the RDF.

Although the establishment of RDF holds good prospects in terms of making additional funds available for sanitation, many questions remain unclear. In particular: Who would be eligible for funding: e.g. could WSCs apply? Which sectors will it cover? Would there be a possibility to earmark funding for specific sectors? How much funding is envisaged in total and from which funding sources? How will the project proposals for funding be ranked? Would joint projects from more than one municipality get extra points?

Committed EU funding

The EU has adopted a package of EUR 41 million to support civil society, regional development and agriculture in Armenia. This assistance is being provided in the framework of the European Neighbourhood Policy. The programme consists of three parts, including *Support to Regional Development in Armenia* to ensure progress towards the more balanced social and economic development between regions of Armenia (EUR 10 million).[3]

Eastern Europe Energy Efficiency and Environment Partnership (E5P)

The E5P is a EUR 93 million multi-donor Fund initiated during the Swedish Presidency of the EU in 2009 to encourage investment in energy efficiency and environmental projects in Ukraine with the intention to include other Eastern Partnership countries. In 2012, the E5P Contributors decided to expand the initiative to Moldova, Georgia, Armenia and Azerbaijan. Managed by the EBRD, the Fund merges financial contributions from the EU and a group of over ten nations (from the EU and participating countries) to provide access to both loans and grants for municipal sector projects. The grant allocation criteria are flexible and aim to reduce energy use, pollution and greenhouse gas emissions while avoiding market distortion and increasing competitiveness. The E5P participates in projects as a co-financier. Donor contributions are used as grants to complement loans provided by six international Implementing Agencies: EBRD, EIB, IFC, Nordic Environment Finance Corporation (NEFCO), Nordic Investment Bank (NIB) and the World Bank. Within its first 24 months, 16 projects have been approved.

The E5P operates on the principle that the recipient countries are also contributors to the Fund. Armenia has signed a letter of commitment on 30 May, 2013, with the expectation to become a recipient country by the end of 2014. It is envisioned that the government will contribute to the Fund via the R2E2. The pipeline of projects that have already been discussed is worth approximately EUR 45 million. A Guarantee scheme is planned. It is likely that Armenia will receive funding from the E5P for water, wastewater and solid waste management. The planning conference highlighted the need for municipal reform, however, prior to significant funding being awarded.

The establishment of E5P and the inclusion of Armenia as a recipient country is a positive development. However, communities that are not served by a sewerage network, and especially those which fall outside the service area of the WSCs, will have limited chances to benefit from it due to co-funding requirements. The E5P funding should be made available for joint inter-municipal projects, particularly for the adoption of innovative technologies, for instance treatment systems involving recovery of gas produced during anaerobic digestion.

Table 3.2. **Existing and planned funds – potential for sanitation**

Fund	What is it and how it works	Potential to be used as a channel to finance sanitation
Existing		
Armenian Social Investment Fund (ASIF)	• Grant money channelled to local governments, community organisations and NGOs to rehabilitate basic infrastructure, including "Sanitation and Environmental Infrastructure" (renovation, rehabilitation and construction of sewerage systems) • Demand-driven approach: community involvement in the definition and identification of the microproject and in their supervision • IDA funding has been the main source of funding for ASIF, reaching USD 33.2 million so far	• Soon to become the Regional Development Fund (RDF) • Current application procedures do not prioritise sanitation • Funding should be made available for the poorest and other communities currently without sewerage and sewage treatment. • Funding could also be made available for improved faecal sludge management systems from on-site systems
Renewable Resources and Energy Efficiency Fund (R2E2)	• Established by the Government as an independent NGO. Its main objective is to facilitate investments in the energy sector • Supports the commercialisation of energy projects, typically small-scale, and finances these through banks and other lending institutions	• Has implemented a World Bank-funded project, involving a sanitation component: Yerevan WWTP modernisation (the objective was to increase the wastewater volume for energy generation) • R2E2 should make funding available for sanitation investments based on the potential for developing biogas usage for energy production
The Hayastan All-Armenian Fund (non-governmental)	• Dedicated to sustainable development in Armenia • Financial resources are obtained through fundraising activities • Activities include the construction or renovation of roads, schools, kindergartens, hospitals, and water and gas networks, as well as assistance to socially vulnerable groups	• As a key infrastructure area, sanitation should be a priority area, particularly for rural communities lacking improved facilities • Difficult to see how to influence the Fund's Board of Trustees when determining their activities. A national campaign for sanitation, on the basis of a defined strategy, can help make sanitation a more prominent issue
Planned		
Regional Development Fund (RDF)	• Objectives: implement projects aimed at socio-economic development of the regions using PPPs; build the financial and institutional capacities of local communities; foster Inter-municipal Co-operation; provide investment capital • GoA proposes to allocate 1% of the state budget annually to the RDF • Additional financing could come from international loans and grants and contributions by the local governments	• Great potential to be used for financing sanitation • Plans to establish the RDF are still in initial stages, however, and there are uncertainties regarding the sectors that the Fund will cover. What will the funding mechanism be? What will the selection criteria be? • It would be necessary to foster Inter-Municipal Co-operation for sanitation investments to increase the possibility of getting funding from the RDF
Eastern Europe Energy Efficiency and Environment Partnership (E5P)	• Objectives: reduce energy use, pollution and greenhouse gas emissions • EUR 93 million multi-donor Fund; recipient countries are also contributors to the Fund • Loans and grants for municipal sector projects	• Inclusion of Armenia within E5P country recipient is a positive development regarding sanitation. However, communities without sewerage will have limited chances to benefit from it due to co-funding requirements. • E5P funding should be made available for joint inter-municipal projects, particularly for the adoption of innovative technologies

Source: Authors' own elaboration.

Creating a dedicated fund for sanitation?

Even with the establishment of the RDF, there is a significant risk that funding for sanitation will not be prioritised, given the vast list of infrastructure needs that need to be funded.

In order to ensure that dedicated funding goes to sanitation, one option would be to create a separate fund for sanitation, what is referred to in this report as the Armenian National Sanitation Fund (ANSF). The proposed ANSF would focus on rural areas so as to enable them to invest in wastewater collection, disposal and other sanitation services.

Precedents of such institutions focused on channelling funding for rural services exist in many countries and sectors (such as for rural electrification or the extension of telecommunication services). For example, France set up a fund for the extension of rural water and sanitation services in 1954, the *Fonds National des Adductions d'Eau* (FNDAE).

Box 3.1. National Fund for Development of Water Supply and Sanitation (FNDAE), France

The National Fund for Development of Water Supply and Sanitation was created in France in 1954 to help rural municipalities with the development of their water and sanitation services. It is managed by the Ministry of Agriculture and was incorporated in 2000 into the National Water Fund. Financial resources for the fund are raised from an additional charge to the water bill as well as from a tax on the revenues from the mutual horse racing betting system established at national level. The fund therefore contains a cross-subsidising element. Its annual budget is about EUR 145 million. Subsidies also come from the departmental local authorities and in certain cases from municipalities with fewer than 3 000 inhabitants.

Revenues from the fund can be used for water and sewerage network extensions, as well as to reduce diffuse pollution from agricultural sources or to repair flood damages on water and sanitation infrastructure.

Source : OECD/Kommunalkredit Public Consulting (2009), *Report on measures to cope with over-fragmentation in the water supply and sanitation sector*, p.36 and www.fndae.fr.

Sources of funds could include domestic public resources (based on the assumption that the Government has understood the critical importance of prioritising sanitation), private funding (from Corporate Social Responsibility, or foundations), fees from environmental fines and penalties as well as donor funding (either on a grant or repayable funding basis.

The ANSF could also provide a financing mechanism for supporting poor households that are looking to acquire improved on-site sanitation facilities. Poor households tend to reside in the poor communities, where local governments are financially too weak to provide such assistance.

The ANSF could also channel funding based on results effectively achieved (and independently verified) to increase the effectiveness of these grants. The potential benefits of a results-based financing (RBF) approach would be as follows:

- fosters a performance-based approach in sector as a whole

- subsidies tend to be lower (competitive application process)

- subsidies better targeted on the poor or results that matter for society as a whole (e.g. environmental clean-up)

- subsidies are only disbursed if results are achieved.

This could result in substantial savings when compared to providing upfront subsidies, as there is a strong risk with the latter that funds allocated based on inputs may not be spent or inadequately spent.

There may be downsides to establishing a separate fund for sanitation, however, which will need to be considered. There will be additional administrative costs associated with its initial set-up and ongoing operation and the fund will have to compete for donor agency funding. The Fund will also take some time to be established, so this might delay funding for sanitation (as opposed to using an existing funding channel).

An alternative could be to earmark funding for sanitation within other funding channels, such as the planned RDF. If this option is retained, funding from the future RDF should be made available not only to communities, but also to businesses as well as NGOs. This would be a major departure from the way in which the ASIF has operated until this point, but in line with similar experience from RDFs in similar countries (such as Moldova). This would allow for businesses willing to engage in the management of improved on-site sanitation or local wastewater treatment solutions (especially for joint intercommunity projects) to obtain the funding that they need to engage. This is not currently available to them from the banks or microfinance institutions. Alternatively, a Sanitation Fund would be able to provide such funding.

The establishment of Local Environmental Funds (for one or more communities) should be encouraged. The idea of such funds is under discussion in Armenia (led by the Ministry of Nature Protection). The main concept is that the environmental fees and fines would be paid into such funds rather than to the central budget and thereafter used for funding environmental projects in the affected localities, thus assuring the implementation of the "Polluter-Pays" principle. There is no final decision as yet about these reforms, however. Such funds would enable making funding available for WSS projects at the local level for the communities outside the service area of the WSCs. Such funding is still likely to be limited, particularly for sanitation, as a focus on water investments is likely to prevail.

Environmental fiscal reform should be accelerated with a special attention for sanitation. The Ministry of Nature Protection is designing environmental fiscal reform measures, including reforming the level and structure of water abstraction and environmental fees and establishing a water component in the land and property tax/renting system in the vicinity of Lake Sevan.

Another option would be to establish a joint Fund for Environmental Protection and Sanitation jointly under the MTA and the MNP. The tentatively planned Local Environmental Funds (which could be renamed Local Environment and Sanitation Funds) could be under the supervision of the suggested joint central Fund.

The Government should also develop a guide for prioritisation of WSS projects, which will address sanitation specifically. The guide would be used particularly in situations in which public funds were involved. There will be competing demands for such public funds. The justifications for the need of the funding will relate to their environmental benefits, health impact, economic gains, etc. The projects will vary in size and in the resources required. The funders will need to be able to choose between several projects related to sanitation. Having a country wide Sanitation Masterplan will be the first starting point in enabling such prioritisation (individual projects will need to be in line with it to be eligible). The Government, with IFI support, should set training as well as TA schemes for the communities (partly funded and channelled for example through the PIU of the SCWS).

Leveraging private funds: Commercial banks and microfinance organisations

Unlike in the energy sector, there is currently no concessional lending programme for sanitation: whether for wastewater treatment equipment for businesses or for households to acquire improved on-site sanitation. Several IFIs implement RE projects in Armenia via loans to the commercial banks for concessional on-lending. Most of these interventions target Small Hydro Power Projects (SHPPs). The EBRD is currently funding a programme that is not explicitly targeting SHPPs, with USD 20 million lent to Ameria Bank and Anelik Bank for on-lending for RE and EE investments for private companies. In reality, however, this programme almost exclusively funded SHPPs. The research carried out under the project on developing the "Roadmap for the Development of Renewable Energy" identified many barriers on the way of developing RE potential, other than small HPPs. These include the lack of specialists within the banks for assessing applications other projects related to RE which would relate to sanitation (e.g. biomass).

There are a number of microcredit organisations in Armenia, including: FINCA (www. finca.am), Aregak (www.aregak.am), and Kamurj (www.kamurj.am). Some of these, e.g. FINCA, have received loans both from IFC and EBRD for on-lending. However, sanitation investments have not been prioritised. The funding terms do not include credit products tailored for sanitation, but rather for SMEs and agriculture. As with commercial banks, it should be expected that these organisations would lack the capacity to appraise loan applications for sanitation.

The Government should establish procedures for commercial banks' lending to communities in order to fully legitimise the process. In parallel, parts of IFIs-funded concessional credit lines should be dedicated to local wastewater treatment plants. A training programme on the assessment of project proposals should accompany such initiatives. Similar schemes are also needed for private entrepreneurs who would want to engage in the business of installing and managing improved on-site sanitation solutions.

Notes

1. www.armeniasif.am/index.php.

2. www.himnadram.org/index.php?id=2.

3. http://europa.eu/rapid/press-release_IP-13-1303_en.htm.

References

Torres, A. (2013), *Armenia: Fostering the Long-Term Financial Viability and Sustainability of the Armenian Water and Sewerage Company*, Asian Development Bank, Working Paper Series, No. 4., Mandaluyong.

Community Finance Officers' Association of Armenia (2005), *Study on Infrastructure Development Projects, in Rural Areas of Armenia*, Yerevan.

European Neighbourhood Policy Instrument (2011), *Shared Environmental Information Systems, Armenia Country Report*, Yerevan.

Manvelyan, E. (2012), *Ecological Sanitation in Rural Armenia*, Yerevan.

Ministry of Economy of the RoA (2013), *Armenia Development Strategy for 2013-2025*, Revised Final Draft, Yerevan.

OECD/Kommunalkredit Public Consulting (2009), *Report on measures to cope with over-fragmentation in the water supply and sanitation sector*, p.36.

Chapter 4

Accompanying legal and regulatory changes for sanitation in Armenia

This chapter describes the current legal and contractual framework for sanitation services in Armenia and discusses the potential changes required to drive reform. The absence of comprehensive legal act to regulate the sanitation sector in Armenia is discussed and the need for the case for separation of sanitation related legislation in the water code presented. The chapter also describes the changes required for contractual frameworks for private sector operators and presents the case for the need for model contracts.

Current legal and contractual framework and its limitations

There is no unified comprehensive legal act to regulate the sanitation sector at present. The regulation of sanitation services is defined, with water supply in mind and therefore indirectly, by several sets of laws in the Constitution and the 2002 Water Code. Legal acts in relation to sanitation, including by-laws, governmental decrees, decisions of the PSRC, legal acts of the State Committee of Water Systems (SCWS) of the MTA, legal acts of municipalities, are adopted on the basis of the Constitution and the Water Code.

The main principles in the Water Code applicable to sanitation include:

- The system of Water System Use Permits (WSUPs), which constitute compulsory licences for all water and sanitation services. WSUPs regulate non-competitive water supply systems management and tariffs.

- Water should be treated as a heritage, to be protected, conserved and used in ways that take into account the interests of future generations.

- Increasing the efficiency of water supply and sanitation systems.

A consolidated legislation that captures all requirements relating to sanitation services is currently lacking. WSUPs can contribute to improving monitoring and control and accountability of WSCs, but they cannot per se ensure overall improvement of sanitation services. They need to be supported and supplemented with relevant legal regulations at the level of normative legal acts. Furthermore, monitoring and enforcement of the requirements under the WSUPs needs to be improved.

Explicit separation of sanitation-related legislation in the Water Code

In order to accelerate sanitation sector reforms, it is necessary to carry out reforms of the legal framework. One reasonable option would be to develop a new Chapter in the Water Code for sanitation.

The development of a new chapter in the Water Code will facilitate simultaneous improvements to the other provisions of the Water Code related to the sanitation sphere. This new Chapter in the Water Code can be relatively easily connected with the mentioned legislation avoiding discrepancies, conflicts and duplication of provisions.

Amongst other areas, the new Chapter in the Water Code should deal with actions to be taken to deal with the issues identified in the sanitation strategy. These might include the following:

- Establish the process for LSGBs to select the most appropriate technical and managerial option for their sanitation services.

- Define principles for setting wastewater tariffs in a cost-covering manner with clear and transparent rules about cross-subsidies.

- Adopt measures that can strengthen enforcement of environmental controls, such as stronger penalties for illegal discharges.

- Develop and adopt "Rules for receiving industrial wastewater into municipal wastewater system". These rules will regulate the qualitative and quantitative indicators of industrial wastewater discharged into the municipal wastewater systems, as well as the mechanisms regulating the issues of violation of the indicators and compensation for the caused damage.

- Establish the Armenia National Sanitation Fund.

- Draft rules related to the installation and operation of individual pit toilets, individual compact treatment plants, monitoring, permissions and rules of the reuse of treated wastewater and sludge.

In addition, changes in the contractual frameworks for the private sector operators must be introduced. The Contracts of all specialised operators expire next year and new contract(s) will be signed in 2016 with one or two operators depending on which market structure reform option is adopted. The new private sector operator contract is likely to be a leasing contract.

It is recommended that the new contracts be drafted with the needs of the sanitation sector in mind, reflecting the planned roles of WSCs in the area of sewerage but also faecal sludge management. For example, targets for sewerage network expansion should be included in the asset-holding company contract and for sewage treatment in WSC's future contracts.

Crucially the legal framework for inter-municipal co-operation has not yet been set out, despite a Strategy on Community Consolidation and the Establishment of Inter-Community Unions. However, such legal framework would help incentivise local governments to seek partnerships.

Adequate legal framework to enable IMC

According to Article 78 of the Law of RA "On local self-governance", for the purpose of jointly resolving various community problems and reducing expenses, the local self-government bodies may form intercommunity associations. The intercommunity associations shall have the status of a legal entity. The objectives and competence of intercommunity associations are established by law. So far, there is no legal act adopted to set up the design and the structure of such entities, however. Subsequently, in practice, such associations don't exist in the manner and form provided in the law. Current intercommunity associations if any are registered as NGOs, which doesn't ensure sufficient efficiency both in terms of investments and economic flexibility. Current tax legislation does not make any distinction between the mentioned and other legal entities as there is no consistent legal scheme to address needs and peculiarities of intercommunity associations. To this end, it is worth to mention, that even in case of establishment of commercial legal entities (LLC, JSC or co-operative), the tax regime is not in favour, under current legislation.

Contractual arrangements between communities

Communities that have joined an ICU or signed a contract could be left vulnerable and uncertain with regards to business decisions if the legal framework remains unclear. An adequate legal structure for IMC development should therefore include:

- a law on inter-municipal co-operation (the need for such a law is stipulated in the strategy for the development of IMC)

- bylaws regulating identification, planning and implementation of municipal improvements

- regulations on sources of revenues of the inter-municipal unions

- regulations on types of expenditures of the inter-municipal unions

- regulations on contributions to the inter-municipal unions.

In the meantime, in the absence of such laws and regulations, to ensure that the suggested contracts between communities are effective, the following areas should at least be elaborated:

- Governance arrangements: how to allocate voting rights among participating local governments.

- Conditions required to join and to withdraw from the association/agreement, specifying the conditions of claiming the assets created under the association.

- Regime of assets, specifying the ownership of assets, financing and management of assets created under the association/agreement.

- Agreements on sharing profits and losses among the participating communities.

Model contracts

Regardless of the service organisation's legal form, the relationship between the IMUs and the service provider should be properly regulated. Critical element of this client-contractor relationship is the service contract, which regulates all components of effective service provision. A good service contract has provisions on all of the following critical elements: *(a)* service specification, including customer relations, risk sharing, guarantees used for service failures or even unexpected bankruptcy of the service organisation; *(b)* financing arrangements, including revenue administration responsibilities; and *(c)* the provisions on the agreement itself: how the contract is monitored, what the consequences of non-performing service organisation or non-payment are, and how the disputes are resolved.

The Government could help by developing model contracts for IMUs in sanitation and these could be used in the pilot projects.

References

OECD (2010), *Guidelines for Performance based contracts between water utilities and municipalities: Lessons Learned from Eater Europe, Caucasus and central Asia*, OECD, Paris, https://www.oecd.org/env/outreach/48656736.pdf.

OECD (2008), *Promoting the Use of Performance-Based Contracts between Water Utilities and Municipalities in EECCA Case Study no. 1: Yerevan Water Supply Company Lease Contract*, OECD, Paris, https://www.oecd.org/environment/outreach/40572658.pdf.

Stiggers, D. (2008), PPP International Best Practice and Regional Application: Water & Sanitation, Case Study 2, WBI, Tegucigalpa.

Bibliography

Anakhasyan, E. et al. (2012), *Cross-contamination of distributed drinking water as the cause of waterborne outbreaks in Armenia 1992-2010*, Journal of Water, Sanitation and Hygiene for Development, Vol.2, no 3, IWA Publishing, London, pp 146-156.

AWSC/SAUR (2012), *Annual Reports 2010-2012*.

Armenian Marketing Association NGO, (2011), *Annual Survey of Social Impact of Water Supply and Sanitation services by Yerevan Water WSC*.

Community Finance Officers' Association of Armenia (2005), *Study on Infrastructure Development Projects, in Rural Areas of Armenia*, Yerevan.

EBRD (2005), *Can poor consumers pay for energy and water? An affordability analysis for transition countries*, Fankhauser and Tepic.

Estache, A., Q. Wodon and V. Foster (2002), *Accounting for poverty in infrastructure reform: Learning from Latin America's experience*, World Bank, Washington, DC.

European Neighbourhood Policy Instrument (2011), *Shared Environmental Information Systems, Armenia Country Report*, Yerevan.

EU/Ministry of Nature Protection of Armenia (2011), *Ten Years of Experience in Reforming water management sector in Armenia: towards the EU Water Management Directive*, Transboundary River Management for the Kura River Basin Phase III, Armenia, Georgia and Azerbaijan, ENPI, 281-959.

EU/Urban Foundation for Sustainable Development of Armenia (2012), *Republic of Armenia: Assessment of Existing Urban Development Challenges, Policies and Institutional Capacities*.

Ewing, A. (2003), *Water Quality and Public Health Monitoring of Surface Waters in the Kura-Araks River Basin of Armenia, Azerbaijan, and Georgia*, Water Resources Programme, The University of New Mexico, Albuquerque, New Mexico 87131, Publication No. WRP-8.

Federal Institute for Research on Building, Urban Affairs, and Spatial Development of Germany/DV (2012), *Partnership for sustainable rural-urban development: existing evidences*, no 011.CE.16.0.AT.017, p.53.

Government of Armenia (2012a), *2013-2015 Medium-Term Public Expenditure Framework*, Yerevan.

Government of Armenia (2012), *Rio +20: Republic of Armenia National Assessment Report*, Bavigh Printing House, Yerevan.

Government of Armenia (2010), *Armenia Millennium Development Goals. National Progress Report, 2005-2009*.

International Monetary Fund (2013), Country Report No. 13/34.

Institute for Applied Environmental Economics (2008), *National Policy Dialogue on Financing Strategy for Rural water supply and Sanitation in Armenia*, Amsterdam.

Institute of Economic Research (2004), *The Role of Communities in Regulating Public Utilities, Public Communal Services and Irrigation: Comparative analysis, Armenia – South Caucasus – Central and Eastern European Countries*, funded by Local Government Initiative/ Open Society Institute, Yerevan.

Kachvoryan, E. et al. (2008), *Ecosystems of Lake Sevan Basin's Rivers in Armenia*, World Academy of Science, Engineering and Technology 44.

Manvelyan, E. (2012), *Ecological Sanitation in Rural Armenia*, Yerevan.

Ministry of Economy of the RoA (2013), *Armenia Development Strategy for 2013-2025*, Revised Final Draft, Yerevan.

Ministry of Economy of the RoA (2011a), *Strategy of Export-Led Industrial Policy of the RoA*.

Ministry of Economy of the RoA (2011b), *Concept Paper on the Development of Tourism in Armenia*.

Ministry of Energy and Natural Resources (2012), *MTEF for 2013-2015*.

Ministry of Territorial Administration (2011), *Concept Paper on Territorial Development*.

Ministry of Health, Armenia (2011), *Water pollution prevention, and control in Armenia*.

Ministry of Nature Protection (2011), *Introduction of Payment for Ecosystem Management Services Schemes in Upper Hrazdan Pilot River Basin of Armenia*, Geoinfo" Ltd; October, 2011.

Ministry of Nature Protection (2010), *Second National Communication Under the United Nations Framework Convention on Climate Change*.

Ministry of Nature Protection (2009), *Vulnerability of water resources in the Republic of Armenia under Climate Change*.

MVV (2011), *LSN utility management*, Annual Reports, 2011, 2012.

National Statistics Service of the RoA (2012a), *Preliminary Results of the 2011 Census*, Yerevan.

National Statistics Service of the RoA (2012b), *Statistical yearbook 2011*, Yerevan.

National Statistics Service of the RoA (2012c), *Environment and Natural Resources in the Republic of Armenia for 2011*, Yerevan.

National Statistics Service of the RoA (2012d), *Social Snapshot and poverty in Armenia in 2011*, Yerevan.

National Statistics Service of the RoA (2012e), *Housing resources and public utility of the Republic of Armenia for 2011*, Yerevan.

National Statistics Service of the RoA (2012f), *Marzes of the Republic of Armenia and Yerevan city in figures in 2011*, Yerevan.

National Statistics Agency of Armenia (2011), *Demographic and Health Survey 2010*, Yerevan.

Nazaryan, G. (2012), *GEO Alaverdi: Environment and Urban Development*, OSCE Yerevan Office, ISBN 978-9939-50-113-0.

Petikuyan, A. (2012), *Water pollution prevention and control in Armenia*, Ministry of Health, presentation.

Policy Forum Armenia (2010), *The State of Armenia's Environment*, Yerevan.

OECD (2010a), *Innovative Financing Mechanisms for the Water Sector*, OECD, Paris.

OECD (2010b), *Guidelines for Performance based contracts between water utilities and municipalities: Lessons Learned from Eater Europe, Caucasus and central Asia*, OECD, Paris, https://www.oecd.org/env/outreach/48656736.pdf.

OECD (2008a), *National Policy Dialogue on Financing Strategy for Rural Water Supply and Sanitation in Armenia*, OECD, Paris.

OECD (2008b), *Promoting the Use of Performance-Based Contracts between Water Utilities and Municipalities in EECCA Case Study no. 1: Yerevan Water Supply Company Lease Contract*, OECD, Paris, https://www.oecd.org/environment/outreach/40572658.pdf.

OECD (2004), *Financing Strategy for Urban Wastewater Collection and Treatment infrastructure in Armenia: Final Report*, OECD, Paris.

OECD/Kommunalkredit Public Consulting (2009), *Report on measures to cope with over-fragmentation in the water supply and sanitation sector*, OECD, Paris.

OECD/EUWI/ACTeon (2013), *Facilitating the Reform of Economic Instruments for Water management in Armenia: Proposed Options for Reform – Assessment of the expected impacts and requisites for implementation*, Vahagn Tonoyan, Gloria De Paoli, Pierre Strosser, National Policy Dialogue Meeting – Yerevan.

OSCE office in Yerevan (2009) *CASE (Civic Action for Security and Environment)*, Small Grants Programme, Strategic plan.

Saghatelyan, A., L.Sahakyana and O. Belyaeva (2012), *Polluted Irrigation Waters as a Risk factor to public health*, Chemistry Journal of Moldova. General, Industrial and Ecological Chemistry. 7 (2), 84-88.

Stiggers, D. (2008), *PPP International Best Practice and Regional Application: Water & Sanitation, Case Study 2*, WBI, Tegucigalpa.

State Committee of Water System under the Ministry of Territorial Administration of the Republic of Armenia (2011), *Public Private Partnerships: Case of Water Infrastructure of the Republic of Armenia*,Yerevan.

Sustainable Sanitation Alliance (2009), *Case study of SuSanA project: UDD toilets in rural school*, Yerevan.

Torres, A. (2013), *Armenia: Fostering the Long-Term Financial Viability and Sustainability of the Armenian Water and Sewerage Company*, Asian Development Bank, Working Paper Series, No. 4., Mandaluyong.

Tumanyan, D. (eds.) (2012) *Local Self-Government Reforms in Armenia: 2011*, Book 4, Communities Finance Officers Association of Armenia, Noyan Tapan, Yerevan.

United Nations Economic Commission for Europe (2010), *Lessons Learned from the Implementation of the Armenian NPD on IWRM*, Geneva.

Urban Foundation for Sustainable Development (2011), *The role of Central Government in Facilitating The Development of Decentralised Water Supply and Sanitation Services: The Case of Armenia.*

USAID Armenia/Counterpart International (2011), *Expanding Opportunities for Financing Local Government Service Delivery and Infrastructure through Public-Private Partnerships*, Civil Society and Local Government Support Programme, CSLGSP.

Veolia Water/Yerevan Water WSC (2012), *Annual reports 2010-2012.*

Vardanyan, M. et al. (2005), *Towards integrated water resources management in Armenia*, in Sustainable Development and Planning II, Vol. 1 773, WIT; Transactions on Ecology and the Environment, Vol 84, WIT Press www.witpress.com, ISSN 1743-3541.

Watson, G. (1995), *Good sewers cheap?: Agency-customer interaction in low-cost urban sanitation in Brazil*, Washington: World Bank.

WHO (2009), *Armenia Country profile: Environmental Burden of Disease", Public Health and the Environment*, Geneva.

WHO (2004), *Energy sustainable development and health, in Chapter 3 of "Access to electricity and heating"*, WHO background papers, Geneva.

World Bank (2011), *Republic of Armenia: Water Sector Note*, Sustainable Development Department Europe and Central Asia Region, Report No. 61317-AM.

World Bank (2006), *Housing and Communal Services in the Southern Caucasus: Multi-Apartment Housing in Armenia, Issues Note*, World Bank, Infrastructure Department, Europe and Central Asia Region.

World Bank (2002). *Sourcebook for poverty reduction strategies, core techniques and cross cutting issues*, Washington, DC.

ORGANISATION FOR ECONOMIC CO-OPERATION AND DEVELOPMENT

The OECD is a unique forum where governments work together to address the economic, social and environmental challenges of globalisation. The OECD is also at the forefront of efforts to understand and to help governments respond to new developments and concerns, such as corporate governance, the information economy and the challenges of an ageing population. The Organisation provides a setting where governments can compare policy experiences, seek answers to common problems, identify good practice and work to co-ordinate domestic and international policies.

The OECD member countries are: Australia, Austria, Belgium, Canada, Chile, the Czech Republic, Denmark, Estonia, Finland, France, Germany, Greece, Hungary, Iceland, Ireland, Israel, Italy, Japan, Korea, Latvia, Luxembourg, Mexico, the Netherlands, New Zealand, Norway, Poland, Portugal, the Slovak Republic, Slovenia, Spain, Sweden, Switzerland, Turkey, the United Kingdom and the United States. The European Union takes part in the work of the OECD.

OECD Publishing disseminates widely the results of the Organisation's statistics gathering and research on economic, social and environmental issues, as well as the conventions, guidelines and standards agreed by its members.

OECD PUBLISHING, 2, rue André-Pascal, 75775 PARIS CEDEX 16
(42 2017 06 1 P) ISBN 978-92-64-26899-9 – 2017